CW00555187

Dublin

by Hilary Weston and
Jackie Staddon

Hilary Weston and Jackie Staddon are freelance
travel writers who have many years of
experience writing and editing travel guides. Their
love of Ireland has taken them there on many
occasions and they have contributed to several
books on Dublin and the Emerald Isle. Other AA
books they have contributed to include *Essential
Rome, Essential Gran Canaria, CityPack London*
and *CityPack Florence.* They are also the authors
of *CityPack Milan.*

Georgian architecture (above)

AA Publishing

*Street musicians in
Grafton Street*

Written by Hilary Weston and Jackie Staddon

First published 2005.

© Automobile Association Developments Limited 2005

Published by AA Publishing, a trading name of Automobile
Association Developments Limited, whose registered office is
Southwood East, Apollo Rise, Farnborough, Hampshire,
GU14 0JW. Registered number 1878835.

Automobile Association Developments Limited retains the
copyright in the original edition © 2005 and in all subsequent
editions, reprints and amendments.

Maps based on Ordnance Survey Ireland Permit No. 7896
© Ordnance Survey Ireland and Government of Ireland

A CIP catalogue record for this book is available from the
British Library.

Find out more about
AA Publishing and the
wide range of travel
publications and services
the AA provides by
visiting our website at
www.theAA.com/bookshop

A01997

Colour separation: Keenes, Andover
Printed and bound in Italy by Printer Trento S.r.l

Contents

About this Book

This book is divided into five sections to cover the most important aspects of your visit to Dublin.

Viewing Dublin pages 5–14
An introduction to Dublin by the authors.
    Dublin's Features
    Essence of Dublin
    The Shaping of Dublin
    Peace and Quiet
    Dublin's Famous

Top Ten pages 15–26
The authors' choice of the Top Ten places to see in Dublin, listed in alphabetical order, each with practical information.

What to See pages 27–90
Two sections: Dublin and Around Dublin, each with its own brief introduction and an alphabetical listing of the main attractions.
    Practical information
    Snippets of 'Did you know…' information
    4 suggested walks
    2 suggested tours
    2 features

Where To… pages 91–116
Detailed listings of the best places to eat, stay, shop, take the children and be entertained.

Practical Matters pages 117–124
A highly visual section containing essential travel information.

Maps
All map references are to the individual maps found in the What to See section of this guide.
For example, Dublin Castle has the reference ✚ 28C3 – indicating the page on which the map is located and the grid square in which the castle is to be found. A list of the maps that have been used in this travel guide can be found in the index.

Prices
Where appropriate, an indication of the cost of an establishment is given by € signs:
€€€ denotes higher prices, €€ denotes average prices, while € denotes lower charges.

Star Ratings
Most of the places described in this book have been given a separate rating:

✪✪✪   Do not miss
✪✪   Highly recommended
✪   Worth seeing

Viewing
Dublin

The impressive exterior of the Four Courts (above)
Joining in the St Patrick's Day Parade (right)

5

The Authors' Dublin

The *Craic*
The *craic*, pronounced 'crack', is synonymous with Ireland and the Irish. It doesn't just mean a good chat but is an all-encompassing word that relays the essence of a good time. It's a mood, something in the air....people, events and places can all be called great '*craic*'. It usually contains certain elements: friends, music, drink, laughter and, of course, that all-important Irish atmosphere.

A street artist at work on Earl Street (below). Enjoying the St Patrick's Day Parade (bottom)

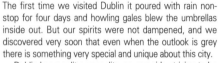

The first time we visited Dublin it poured with rain non-stop for four days and howling gales blew the umbrellas inside out. But our spirits were not dampened, and we discovered very soon that even when the outlook is grey there is something very special and unique about this city.

Dublin has a split personality, on one side striving to be cosmopolitan, but on the other still rough around the edges. It can be calm and soothing or lively and exhilarating; chic and modern with trendy bars and high-flying young people, or old-fashioned with traditional pubs and an older generation still hanging on to pre-EU values. It takes only a few days of wandering round to get to know Dublin intimately. Dubliners still bump into people they know on the street; imagine the chances of that happening in London or Paris. Despite some exceptional Georgian architecture, it can look dull and grey, but only a few stops away on the DART and you can be by the sea or among spectacular mountain scenery.

What was it on that wet and windy visit to Dublin that really got under our skin? Its fascination, without doubt, lies within the people. They are laid back, have a great sense of humour and love to stop for a chat. There is a twinkle in the eye, an impish grin and irresistible charm that is uniquely Irish.

With a booming economy, Dublin is ever-changing and as the surge of partying visitors and sophisticated bars and restaurants continue to shape the city, we sincerely hope that the old Dublin will hold its ground.

Dublin's Features

Geography

- Dublin, the capital city of the Republic of Ireland, is situated on the Irish Sea at the mouth of the River Liffey and covers an area of 115sq km (44 square miles).
- Greater Dublin's limits are Howth to the north and Bray Head to the south.
- There are two main canals running through the city, the Royal and the Grand.
- Dublin is the driest area of Ireland, with a maximum annual rainfall of 750mm (30 inches), and has mild winters and cool summers.
- The average temperature is 16–20°C (60–68°F) in summer and 4–7°C (39–44°F) in winter.
- Just to the south of the city are the Wicklow Mountains, whose highest point is Lugnaquilla at 926m (3,038ft).

Population

- The population of Greater Dublin is just over 1.1 million while the total population of the Republic of Ireland is 3.9 million.
- Prior to the famines of the mid-19th century, the population of the whole of Ireland was around 8.5 million.
- Over 47 per cent of people in the Republic of Ireland live within 90km (56 miles) of Dublin.
- Approximately 43 per cent of the population is under 25.

Bridges

- The first fordable crossing over the River Liffey was on the site of the present-day Father Matthew Bridge at Merchants' Quay.
- The most famous bridge is the 1816 Ha'penny Bridge (► 49), now restored to its original cream colour.
- More recent bridges include the Millennium Bridge of 2000 and the James Joyce Bridge of 2003, linking Ellis Quay with Usher Island, a dramatic and contemporary addition to Dublin's infrastructure.
- A swing bridge is under construction at Custom House Quay and is due to open in 2005.

Some More Statistics

- Dublin Bus carries some 200 million passengers a year.
- Around 14 million people a year use Dublin Airport.
- The DART (Dublin Area Rapid Transport) carries around 80,000 passengers a day.
- Opened in 2004, the LUAS light rail is hoped to relieve congestion in the city by enabling people to leave their cars at home.
- Car ownership among Dubliners increased tenfold between 1996 and 1998.
- In 1672 there were 1,180 ale houses and 93 breweries in the city; by 1999 this had dropped to 850 pubs and only one major brewer – Guinness.

Georgian architecture in Mount Street (below).
The Millennium Bridge (bottom)

Essence of Dublin

Dublin offers everything you would expect from a capital city – elegant architecture, superb museums, vibrant cultural life, great restaurants – and it is a fantastic place to party. Its close proximity to lush green mountains and coastal towns adds to the appeal. In a city that has suffered a turbulent and often oppressed past, Dubliners have retained a strong sense of pride and identity that, together with their charming and witty character, makes them impossible to resist. With money from the EU to help regenerate the city and a booming economy, even more restaurants and trendy bars are opening up alongside the many traditional pubs. Without doubt, Dublin is having fun and the *craic* is flowing. Give it a try; you won't be disappointed.

Flower stall on Grafton Street (below). Relaxing at the Café en Seine in Dawson Street (bottom)

THE 10 ESSENTIALS

If you only have a short time to visit Dublin, or would like to get a really complete picture of the city, here are the essentials:

• **Visit Kilmainham Gaol** (► 21) to learn about the struggle for Irish independence and appreciate what life was like for the prisoners.

• **Enjoy a music session** and a bit of *craic* in the pub and you'll soon realise how important tradition is to Dubliners.

• **Drink a pint of Guinness at the top of the Guinness Storehouse** (► 19) in the Gravity Bar. The view is breathtaking and the pint comes free with your ticket, a great culmination to the fascinating story of brewing the 'black stuff'.

• **Window-shop on Grafton Street, with a coffee at Bewley's** (► 33) – Dublin's most famous tea room in the smart end of town.

• **Walk the Liffey Quays** along the north-side boardwalk for great views of the river and some of the best examples of grand Georgian buildings.

• **Ride the DART** both north and south along Dublin Bay. In minutes you are out of the city and rattling alongside the coast.

• **Soak up the atmosphere in Temple Bar** (► 71) over a pint, a glass of wine or a cappuccino, or just watch the street entertainers in the square.

• **Stroll around the Georgian district** to view the doorways painted in a variety of colours and topped by picturesque fanlights and wrought iron balconies above.

• **Buy a Dublin Pass**, the best way to see all the main attractions at a reduced rate. Contact the tourist office for the 1-, 2-, 3- or 6-day passes.

• **Take a guided literary walk or a ghost tour** to see the less obvious side of the city. Try the literary pub crawl, the Walk Macabre or the Dublin Ghost Bus for a chilling experience.

Kilmainham Gaol has housed some of Ireland's most famous rebels

The Temple Bar pub (below).
Inside the Guinness Storehouse (bottom)

The Shaping of Dublin

Detail of a mural outside the Setanta Centre in Nassau Street

AD 2
A bridge is built over the River Liffey by the Celts, giving Dublin its Gaelic name 'Åth Cliath' or 'the ford of the hurdles'.

AD 450
St Patrick brings Christianity to Ireland. According to legend he baptised people at St Patrick's Well, in the grounds of St Patrick's Cathedral in the city.

AD 841
A permanent Viking settlement, known as a *longphort*, is established in the area now known as Dublin.

1014
During the battle of Clontarf, high king Brian Boru defeats the Dublin Vikings.

1170
The Irish king Diarmait MacMurchada, together with Norman allies led by Richard de Clare (Strongbow), captures Dublin and by 1172 Christ Church Cathedral is being re-built by the Normans.

1204
Construction of Dublin Castle and the city walls begins.

1348
The Black Death appears in Howth, County Dublin. The disease claims a third of Dublin's population over the next three years.

1487
Lambert Simnel, a pretender to the English throne, is crowned King of England in Dublin's Christ Church Cathedral by Irish leaders.

1536
Parliament in Dublin declares Henry VIII the official head of the Church in Ireland, following his break with Rome.

1592
Queen Elizabeth I's charter instigates the founding of Trinity College to be a seat of Protestant learning.

1660
Charles II is restored to the English throne. After Oliver Cromwell's ill treatment of the Irish people, Dublin prospers and by the early 1700s the population has expanded from 40,000 to 172,000.

1710
Work starts on Trinity College Library and in 1702 the Mansion House, residence of the Lord Mayor, is built.

1759
Arthur Guinness founds the Guinness Brewery, bringing employment that continues to the present day.

1782
The Irish Parliament gains independence from Britain.

1800
The Act of Union is passed and the Irish Parliament is dissolved, pre-empting a period of urban decline.

1847
The Great Potato Famines begin, lasting until 1851. Soup kitchens are set up around the city.

1916
The Easter Rising. The City Hall, General Post Office and other main buildings in the city are taken by the rebels wnting independence from Britain.

1921
After the War of Independence the Anglo-Irish Treaty is signed, partitioning the Irish Free State from Northern Ireland. Civil war follows the next year.

1937
The Irish constitution renames the country Eire and Roman Catholicism is declared the majority religion. In 1949 the country is declared the Republic of Ireland.

1973
Ireland joins the EEC, later known as the European Union.

1979
The Pope takes Mass in Phoenix Park before more than 1.3 million people.

1991
The inaugeration of Ireland's first female president, Mary Robinson. Dublin is European City of Culture.

1996
Ireland holds the Presidency of the European Union for the third time. The European Summit meets in Dublin.

2002
The euro becomes the official currency of Ireland.

2004
The LUAS light rail service comes into operation. In March a no-smoking ban is introduced in public places throughout Ireland.

Queen Victoria visited Dublin in 1900

Peace & Quiet

Enjoying the sunshine at St Stephen's Green

The green spaces and peaceful waterways in and around Dublin are a delightful respite from the hustle and bustle of the city, offering the perfect antidote to traffic congestion, hectic streets and the noise of urban life. Beyond the city, the suburbs soon give way to wonderful coastal, mountain and rolling green scenery.

Parks and Gardens

Popular with Dubliners is the huge open space of Phoenix Park (▶ 65), one of the world's largest urban parks, complete with ancient oaks, wild deer and interesting memorials; it's also home to Dublin Zoo. There are lots more smaller parks and gardens dotted around the city and some have remained relatively wild and unspoilt. Iveagh Gardens (▶ 55) are particularly serene, not far from the more popular St Stephen's Green (▶ 68) with its duck ponds and formal flower beds. Other secret hideaways include the quiet haven at Blessington Street Basin and the small leafy park adjoining St Audoen's Church.

DID YOU KNOW?

According to legend, St Patrick drove all the snakes out of Ireland. In fact, snakes have never been native in the country, but they were a symbol of paganism and it was the pagans St Patrick banished from the land. You can be sure you will never be threatened by snakes when walking in Dublin's parks or in the countryside. Ireland has around 125 species of resident wild birds and 250 species of visiting birds. There are 27 mammal species but only one reptile, the common lizard. There are also no moles in Ireland.

Waterways

Dublin's main watery thoroughfare, the River Liffey, cuts the city in two. A stroll along the riverside boardwalk may not be peaceful but it can be relaxing, and beyond the hectic O'Connell and Ha'penny bridges the crowds thin; here you can pause for a coffee or sit by the water – a pleasant alternative to sightseeing. Dublin's two canals, the Royal and the Grand (➤ 48) offer tranquil walks along the picturesque towpaths.

Beyond the City

The coastal villages north and south of Dublin are easily accessible by the DART in less than half an hour, and there is exceptional coastal scenery along the way. A trip to Howth (➤ 52) will blow the cobwebs away with a bracing walk high above the bay at Howth Head. Or try Dollymount Strand (➤ 41) with its long sandy beach where Dubliners come to paddle, walk their dogs or fly a kite. To the south of the city, but still within easy reach, the magnificent Wicklow Mountains bring you close to nature, away from the urban sprawl.

Taking a stroll through a leafy tree-lined pathway in St Stephen's Green

Flora and Fauna

The gardens of Dublin provide some dazzling floral displays, with particularly fine examples at the National Botanic Gardens (➤ 58) at Glasnevin and at St Anne's Park and Rose Gardens (➤ 66). The huge sweep of Dublin Bay is a magnificent haven for birds; the sanctuary at North Bull Island attracts around 25,000 wading birds resident in winter. Ireland's Eye, the island off Howth Head, has a colony of gannets. Other birds such as cormorants, puffins, razorbills and guillemots may be spotted, and you might even see seals and porpoises. To the south, the bay provides a refuelling stop for migrating birds, with freshwater and saltwater habitats for birds including moorhen, teal, snipe and Brent geese.

Dublin's Famous

Jonathan Swift

Clergyman and satirist Jonathan Swift (1667–1745) was born in Dublin. He studied at Trinity College, moving to

England to become secretary to the diplomat Sir William Temple. During a visit to Ireland in 1695 he was ordained in the Anglican Church and went on to be Dean of St Patrick's Cathedral from 1713 until 1745. During this time he was an ardent advocate of the rights of the Irish people, writing pamphlets and religious and political essays. It is for his satirical works that he is best remembered, most famously *Gulliver's Travels*, often regarded as a children's book, but in reality a powerful exposé of the stupidity of humankind.

James Joyce

DUBLIN AND EAST TOURISM

THE ORMOND HOTEL

IS THE SETTING
FOR THE EPISODE

THE SIRENS
IN
JOYCES ULYSSES

The greatest exponent of the Dublin character among Irish writers, James Joyce (1882–1941) wrote of his home town in novels and short stories such as *Ulysses* and *Dubliners*. His work revolutionized the novel form with his exploration of language and by breaking away from an ordinary plot – using the technique known as the 'stream of consciousness'. He spent much of his adult life abroad, leaving Dublin in 1910 and travelling to Trieste and Zurich, before finally setting up home in Paris.

A sign for The Ormond Hotel (above) details its connection to James Joyce's Ulysses

U2

Ireland's greatest music export and one of the world's most successful rock bands was conceived in 1977 in the Mount Temple School in Dublin. The four school friends first used the name U2 in 1978 and played some of their earliest gigs at the Dandelion Market in Dublin. By the 1980s U2 were well established at the forefront of the local rock scene and it wasn't long before they hit the big time. They went on to perform all over the world, but their roots have stayed firmly in Dublin and they still live, work and play in the city. In 2000 they were awarded Freedom of the City.

Top Ten

*A view of the Gravity Bar at the
Guinness Storehouse (above).
A figure (right) in the Chester
Beatty oriental collection*

1
Christ Church Cathedral

www.cbl.ie

28C3

Christchurch Place

677 8099

Mon–Fri 9:45–5,
Sat–Sun 10–5

Tara Street

Cross-city buses

Good

Moderate

Dvblinia (➤ 44)

*Flags in celebration of
St Patrick's Day decorate
Christ Church Cathedral*

*Dublin's oldest stone building and stronghold of
the Protestant faith in Ireland was saved from
ruin by extensive Victorian restoration.*

Built on the site of the Norse king Sitric Silkenbeard's wooden church of 1038, this Romanesque and early Gothic church was commissioned in 1172 by Richard de Clare, the Anglo-Norman conqueror of Dublin – better known as Strongbow – for Archbishop Laurence O'Toole. The archbishop later became St Laurence, patron of Dublin, whose heart remains in the cathedral in a 13th-century metal casket.

After Henry VIII broke with Rome, Robert Castle, the last prior of the Augustinian priory of Holy Trinity, became the first dean of Christ Church in 1541. In 1562 the nave roof vaulting collapsed, crushing Strongbow's tomb and leaving the cathedral in ruins. Temporary measures to shore up the damage remained in place until the 1870s, and the roof, to the present day, still leans out by 46cm (18 inches). During the 16th and 17th centuries Christ Church's crypt was used as a market, a meeting place and even a pub. Heavy restoration at the expense of Henry Roe, a local whiskey distiller, was undertaken by architect George Edmund Street in the 1870s. Although little remains of the original Norman structure – only the south transept and the crypt – the cathedral was saved from complete decay. Further work took place in the 1980s and 1990s, including the restoration of the 12th-century crypt. This contains an intriguing range of relics and objects, including the old wooden punishment stocks. The exhibition 'Treasures of Christ Church' reflects 1,000 years of history, architecture and worship in Ireland.

2

Dublin Castle and Chester Beatty Library

Situated on a strategic ridge, the castle is at the heart of historic Dublin. Visit the superlative gallery and library in the gardens.

Dublin Castle was the headquarters of British rule for over 700 years. Little remains of the original structure, except for the modified Record Tower (containing the Garda Museum), and the mixture of architectural styles and government offices mask the fact that this was originally a Viking fortress. The castle stands on the site of the black pool or *dubh linn* from which the city took its name.

Following a disastrous fire in 1684, more stately accommodation was built to replace the medieval interior, including the lavish Throne Room, used for state visits and presidential inaugurations, and the Ballroom or St Patrick's Hall, where the ceiling fresco is considered the most important painted ceiling in Ireland. The neo-Gothic Chapel Royal was added in 1807 and displays carved stone likenesses of a hundred British dignitaries. The Undercroft was revealed after excavations in 1990 and can be visited on a tour. Here you will see part of the original Viking fortress and, in the base of the Norman Powder Tower, some of the Viking defensive bank.

The Chester Beatty Library is housed in the Clock Tower Building and displays a rich collection of artistic treasures from the great cultures and religions of the world. The array of manuscripts, prints, icons, books and other objects was bequeathed to the nation in 1956 by Sir Alfred Chester Beatty (1875–1968). This successful American mining magnate became one of the few people to have been made an honorary citizen of Ireland.

Dublin Castle
www.dublincastle.ie

✚ 28C3

✉ Dame Street

☎ 677 7129

🌐 Mon–Fri 10–5, Sat–Sun 2–5. Closed during state business

🍴 Castle Vaults Bistro (€–€€)

🚉 Tara Street

🚌 Cross-city buses

♿ Good; no wheelchair access to Undercroft

✋ Moderate

Chester Beatty Library
www.cbl.ie

✚ 28C3

✉ Dublin Castle

☎ 407 0750

🌐 Mon–Fri 10–5, Sat 11–5, Sun 1–5. Closed Mon, Oct–Apr

🍴 Silk Road Café (€)

🚉 Tara Street

🚌 Cross-city buses

♿ Good

✋ Free

The grand Throne Room at Dublin Castle

3

General Post Office

🕇 29D4

✉ O'Connell Street

☎ 705 7000

🕐 Mon–Sat 8–8

🚇 Tara Street

🚌 Cross-city buses

♿ Few

✋ Free

A significant building in the history of modern Ireland, the GPO was the main stronghold of the Irish Volunteers during the Easter Rising of 1916.

The imposing Palladian-style General Post Office in O'Connell Street was built in 1818, and while it is not one of Dublin's finest Georgian buildings, it is important in the history of Irish independence. It was from the steps of this building that Pádraic Pearse (1879–1916), leader of Irish Nationalism, proclaimed Ireland a republic and no longer subject to British rule. He and his fellow volunteers resisted the British in a siege that lasted a week. Heavy bombardment forced the rebels out and the building was left severely ruined. The leaders of the uprising were rounded up and 16 rebels were executed at Kilmainham Gaol (▶ 21), but the struggle against British rule continued and the siege at the Post Office highlights those years of struggle. The Irish Free State was finally formed five years later in 1921.

The building, headquarters of An Post, the Irish Postal Service, re-opened in 1929. Despite heavy restoration, bullet holes can still be seen on the exterior walls. The building is a cross between a memorial to those who died and an everyday busy post office. Take a look inside at the remarkable bronze statue of the *Death of Cuchulainn* (by Oliver Sheppard, 1935), which depicts the demise of the legendary Irish hero Cuchulainn, and is dedicated to Pearse and the others who died in the Easter Rising. Note also the series of paintings depicting the Rising, in the manner of Communist propaganda posters. The building remains the focus of official parades and a salute is given here at Dublin's annual St Patrick's Day parade.

The impressive statue inside the General post Office

4
Guinness Storehouse

Every visitor to Dublin should sample at least one pint of the 'black stuff'. The Storehouse is the ideal place to do this and learn about its production at the same time.

Guinness is synonymous with Dublin, an institution, a dominant employer in the city for over two centuries and now a household name throughout the world. When Arthur Guinness decided to experiment with the English dark porter ale in 1759, little did he know that 200 years later his surname would be revered the world over. Indeed, the largest producer of Guinness is now Nigeria.

The Storehouse, opened in 2000 on the site of the original St James's Gate brewery, pays homage to the memory of that early discovery. The stunning glass central atrium, an innovative structure built into the listed building, is in the shape of a giant pint glass. The froth at the top of the pint is the Gravity Bar where you can sup your free pint at the end of your self-guided tour while enjoying panoramic views over the city. As you make your way up the pint glass you will go through the various production processes. The heady aroma of roasting hops pervade the air and you can touch and smell the individual ingredients. The water used in the production of Guinness is traditionally believed to come from the River Liffey; in fact it comes from the nearby Grand Canal. Further displays, all well labelled and some interactive, include machinery and transport vehicles. Check out the excellent advertising section, including examples of posters depicting the memorable toucan and the famous 1929 advert proclaiming 'Guinness is Good for You'.

www.guinness-storehouse.com

☩ 28A3

✉ St James's Gate

☎ 408 4800, info line 453 8364

🕐 Daily 9:30–5 (9:30–9, Jul, Aug)

🍴 Gravity Bar, Source Bar, Brewery Bar & restaurant (€–€€)

🚌 51B, 78A, 123

♿ Excellent

💷 Expensive

↔ Shop selling Guinness memorabilia

The Gravity Bar at the Guinness Storehouse enjoys stunning views over Dublin

5
James Joyce
Cultural Centre

🕂 29D5

✉ 35 North Great
George's Street

☎ 878 8547

🕐 Mon–Sat 9:30–5, Sun &
public hols 12:30–5

🚌 Cross-city buses

♿ Few

✋ Moderate; tours of
Joycean Dublin
expensive

↔ Bookshop

*The centre is dedicated to fostering and promoting
awareness of James Joyce's significant contribution
to modern literature. Here you will find all
manner of Joycean memorabilia.*

James Joyce (1882–1941) spent most of his adult life in
Europe, but it was his childhood in Dublin that provided him
with the setting and characters for his novels *Ulysses*,
Finnegans Wake and *Dubliners*. Joyce did not live in this
particular house but in the vicinity, which was at the time a
run-down area with most houses needing repair. In 1982
Senator David Norris restored the 18th-century town house
to its original glory and converted it into a centre of Joycean
study. Among the most interesting exhibits is a fascinating
set of biographies of some 50 characters from the most
famous of Joyce's works, *Ulysses*, written between 1914
and 1921.

The centre organizes walking tours so you can trace the
footsteps of the novel's hero, Leopold Bloom, as he walked
around the city on 16 June, 1904. The year 2004 saw the
centenary celebrations of this event with special Bloomsday
festivities throughout the city and around the world.
Rejoyce 2004 also marked several months of activities and
events based around the great master of the novel.

The James Joyce Centre also shows short films on
Joyce and his Dublin, as well as recordings of him reading
his own novels. A highlight of a visit is the current
connection with members of Joyce's family and his
nephew, Ken Monaghan, shows visitors around the house.
Look out for the murals around the courtyard depicting the
18 chapters of *Ulysses*, painted by Paul Joyce, great-
nephew of James Joyce. You can also see the original door
of No 7 Eccles Street, the fictional home of Leopold Bloom.

*An exhibition room
at the James Joyce
Cultural Centre*

6
Kilmainham Gaol

The gaol provides a moving insight into the grim reality of incarceration in Dublin's notorious prison. It remains a symbol of Ireland's fight for independence.

Inspired by the Bastille in Paris, Kilmainham Gaol was built in 1787, and remained a prison until 1924. It has held some of the most famous rebels in Ireland's history, including those from the rebellions of 1798, 1803, 1848, 1867, 1883 and, most famously, the 1916 Easter Rising. Visits are by guided tour only and start with a video presentation to set the grisly scene. The tour, which takes about 90 minutes, places the historical facts in context, emphasizing that this was a prison for civil as well as political prisoners. Petty criminals were also incarcerated here, including many victims of the Great Famine of 1845–49, when stealing was rife. Up to 7,000 inmates, both men and women, were crammed into the dank and dark cells.

The prison closed in 1910 and was converted into barracks to house troops during World War I, but it was re-opened to receive the insurgents of the 1916 Easter Rising. The public execution of 16 of the rebels that took place here included Joseph Plunkett, who married Grace Gifford just ten minutes before his execution. The last prisoner to be held here in 1924 was Eámon de Valera, who went on to become president of Ireland. The abandoned gaol fell into decay, but because of its exceptional historical interest was restored by volunteer groups in the 1960s.

Among the areas taken in by the tour are the east- and west-wing cell blocks, the chapel, the exercise yard where the rebels were executed and the museum with its grim artefacts and Irish memorabilia.

- ✚ Off map at 28A3
- ✉ Inchicore Road, Kilmainham
- ☎ 453 5984
- 🕐 May–Sep, daily 9:30–5; Oct–Apr, Mon–Sat 9:30–4, Sun & public hols 10–5. Last tour 1 hour before closing
- 🍴 Tea room (€)
- 🚌 51B, 78A, 68, 69, 79
- ♿ Call in advance
- ✋ Moderate
- ↔ Guided tours only – advisable to book

A striking interior view of Kilmainham Gaol

7
National Gallery

www.nationalgallery.ie

✠ 29E2

✉ Merrion Square West and Clare Street

☎ 661 5133

🕐 Mon–Sat 9:30–5:30, Thu 9:30–8:30, Sun 12:30–5:30

🍴 Restaurant and café (€–€€)

🚉 Pearse

🚌 Cross-city buses

♿ Very good

✋ Free; donation required for special exhibitions

↔ Guided tours Sat 3PM, Sun 2, 3 and 4PM

Home to one of Europe's premier collections of Old Masters, the National Gallery also showcases home-grown talent, in particular the works of the Yeats family.

The gallery was established by the state in 1854 and opened its doors to the public in 1864. The building was by designed by Francis Fowke, the architect of the Victoria & Albert Museum in London. Beginning with just 125 paintings, the National Gallery's prime task was to inspire Irish artists of the day. The collection now has over 2,500 paintings and some 10,000 works in different media, including drawings, prints and sculptures.

The building consists of four wings: the original Dargan wing, the Milltown Wing (1899–1903), the Beit Wing (1964–68) and the Millennium Wing (2002), the latter housing a study centre of Irish work – complete with a Jack B Yeats archive – and temporary exhibition galleries.

The collections are vast and can be confusing, so pick up a floor plan to orientate yourself. You may want to single out your own personal favourites rather than wander round each gallery. In the Millennium Wing you will find a multimedia gallery with computer touch screens where you can find out background information on paintings in the collection. Every major European school of painting is represented here. If it's Old Masters you're after, look out for works by Fra Angelico, Titian, Caravaggio, Rembrandt and Canova. Lovers of Impressionism can view works by Monet, Degas, Pissarro, Sisley and others. British artists such as Reynolds and Turner are also represented, as are modern painters up to Picasso.

Finally, there is a great emphasis on Irish art, and the Yeats Museum, opened in 1999, is a testament to this. Among the works of Jack B Yeats are several Dublin cityscapes.

The 19th-century façade of the National Gallery

8
National Museum

Ireland's rich heritage is brought to life in this superb building, one of Dublin's foremost attractions, with some of the best gold artefacts on display in Europe.

The collections are exhibited in a magnificent purpose-built building of 1877. The splendid domed rotunda, which forms the entrance hall, has columns of Irish marble and a mosaic floor depicting the signs of the zodiac. This is the national repository for over 2,000,000 artefacts dating from 7000 BC to the late medieval period.

Beginning with the prehistoric period you will find displays of tools and weaponry from the Stone and Bronze ages. Check out the 13m (42ft) Lurgan longboat. Dating from around 2500 BC, it is Ireland's earliest surviving boat, hewn out of an oak tree. Other artefacts are in excellent condition, preserved in Ireland's peat bogs. The stunning Bronze Age gold jewellery of the 'Ór – Ireland's Gold' exhibition is unmatched in Europe and the styles, surprisingly sophisticated, are still copied today. In the Treasury you can see several 8th-century gems including the Ardagh Chalice, a beautiful, gilded, twin-handled cup, and the stunning Tara brooch, intricately decorated with birds and animals. Look out for the gilt-bronze 12th-century Cross of Cong with its silver wire, crystals and enamelled studs. On the same floor, the Road to Independence exhibition is a vivid portrayal of Ireland's turbulent political history from 1900 to the signing of the Anglo-Irish treaty of 1921.

Upstairs are the Viking Age Ireland and Medieval Ireland 1150–1550 collections, perhaps a little more down to earth after the magnificence of the earlier displays. In late 2005 a new exhibition is due to open, telling the stories of Irish soldiers, their families and civilians affected by war across 450 years.

www.museum.ie

✚ 29E2

✉ Kildare Street

☎ 677 7444

🕐 Tue–Sat 10–5, Sun 2–5

🍴 Café (€)

🚉 Pearse

🚌 Cross-city buses

♿ Ground floor good

✋ Free

↔ Guided tours from main entrance at regular intervals

Inside the grand museum

9
Trinity College and the Book of Kells

www.tcd.ie

✚ 29D3

✉ College Street

☎ College: 608 2320; library 677 2941

🕐 College campus open daily. Old Library and Book of Kells: Jun–Sep, Mon–Sat 9:30–5, Sun 9:30–4:30; Oct–May, noon–4:30

🚉 Tara Street

🚌 Cross-city buses

♿ Good

✋ Campus free; Old Library and Book of Kells expensive

↔ College tours May–Sep. Dublin Experience, a multimedia show May–Sep. Douglas Hyde Gallery for temporary art exhibitions all year

Taking a break: relaxing in Fellow's Square in front of the Old Library (above right)

A Henry Moore sculpture in the square at Trinity College (below)

The oldest university in Ireland houses the Book of Kells, arguably one of the most beautifully illuminated manuscripts in the world.

Trinity College is one of the prime attractions in the city, a peaceful oasis close to the hustle and bustle of modern Dublin. It was founded by Queen Elizabeth I in 1592 in an attempt to bring Protestant education and doctrine to the country and to stop the 'popery' rife in the students of the day. Nothing remains of the original buildings, but following the religious turmoil of the 16th and 17th centuries, a new age of building was instigated during the Protestant era of the 18th century when Parliament funded the college's magnificent new halls.

The main entrance is on College Green, opposite the Bank of Ireland, next to one of the busiest roads in Dublin. On Parliament Square, inside the college's grounds, you will find the 19th-century campanile and the elegant 18th-century Dining Hall and the Chapel. As you walk into Fellows' Square, the buildings, both old and new, blend sympathetically. The Old Library (1732), designed by Thomas Burgh, stands to the west; to the east is Benjamin Woodward's 19th-century carved Museum building; to the south Paul Koralek's New Library (1978). The best way to see the College is to take one of the lively and informative walking tours that start every 15 minutes throughout the summer from Front Square.

Most visitors head for the Old Library to see the magnificent treasures held there. Who could come to Dublin and not visit the Book of Kells, housed in the darkened

The impressive interior of Trinity College's Old Library (left)

Treasury on the ground floor? Written on vellum around AD 800, it is a superbly illustrated transcription of the four Gospels. The exhibition 'Turning Darkness into Light' explains the context of the book and how the monastic scribes produced such a sublime work of art. The decoration of the book is highly intricate and imaginative, with depictions of human figures and animals, and ornamented with abstract patterns, a hallmark of Celtic art. It was discovered in the town of Kells in County Meath, but is thought to have been created by four Irish missionary monks on the island of Iona, off the west coast

Golden globe sculpture outside Trinity College Library (below)

of Scotland. Apparently they fled from the Vikings to Ireland and finished the book in Kells. Two volumes can usually be seen, one opened to show the decorative work and one showing script. Two other manuscripts are also on show – the books of Durrow and Armagh, both dating back to the same era as the Book of Kells and equally ornate.

The Long Room, upstairs from the Treasury, is nearly 65m (213ft) in length and houses around 200,000 books. Every available shelf is crammed full and the middle aisle is decorated with marble busts. In 1860 the roof was raised to incorporate the vast collection. The aura of learning and the smell of old books have a powerful effect. Take a look at the harp on display; believed to be the oldest in Ireland, it dates back to the 15th century and is the harp that appears on Irish coins.

10
St Patrick's Cathedral

www.stpatrickscathedral.ie

28C2

Patrick's Close

475 4817

Mar–Oct, Mon–Sat
9–5:15, Sun 9–10:30,
12:30–2:30, 4:30–6;
Nov–Feb, Mon–Sat 9–5,
Sun 10–11, 12:45–3

Cross-city buses

Good

Moderate

*Knights' relics (above) in St
Patrick's Cathedral (below)*

*St Patrick's is Dublin's second great cathedral and
the largest church in Ireland. It is a paradox that
in a predominately Catholic city and country there
should be two Protestant cathedrals.*

Legend has it that St Patrick passed through Dublin on his
travels in Ireland in the 5th century. A small wooden
church was built on the spot where he converted several
pagans to Christianity. On this same site the Anglo-
Norman first bishop of Dublin, John Comyn, constructed a
stone church, which was upgraded to cathedral status in
1219. It was built in the English Gothic style and finally
completed in 1284. By the 19th century it was in a very
poor state and lay almost derelict among slum housing.
Much of the cathedral was rebuilt and restored between
1860 and 1900, paid for mainly by the Guinness family.

Just inside the building is the grave of one of the
cathedral's most famous sons. The author and reformist
Jonathan Swift (► 14) was dean here from 1713 to 1745
and he tried hard to preserve the building, but to no avail.
The death mask, pulpit, chair and writing table of the great
man are among memorabilia on display. Other highlights
include the largest organ in the country, and you can also
hear the largest peal of bells in Ireland. A particularly interesting memorial is the one to the celebrated blind harpist
Turlough O'Carolan (1670–1730). The exhibition 'Living
Stones' celebrates the cathedral's role in city life and its
place in the history of Dublin. It is important to remember
that St Patrick's is not a museum but very much an active
church and an integral part of city life.

What To See

Eden Quay reflected in the River Liffey (above).
Two children enjoy a ride on the back of a horse (right)

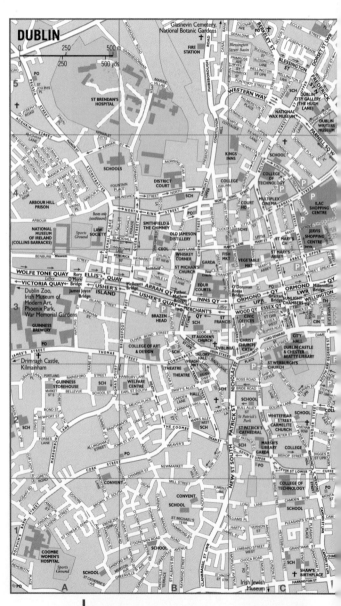

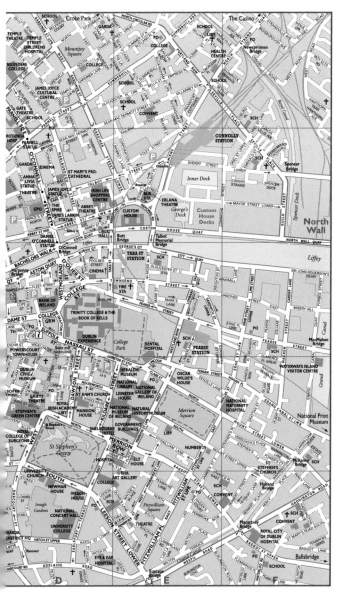

Dublin

Dublin is a small city and very easy to explore. Walking is probably the best option, although there is an excellent bus service. The River Liffey provides a prominent landmark when navigating the city and most attractions are on the south side, including the tourist honeypots of Temple Bar, Grafton Street, Trinity College and the Georgian district, with its renowned national museums and galleries. North of the river has always been considered the poor relation, but with recent restoration projects being carried out at Smithfield Village, O'Connell Street/Henry Street and the docks, these areas are taking on a smarter image. With the influx of EU money, the renovation of Dublin is ongoing, with parts of the city seemingly forever under scaffolding. After dark, serious partygoers head for Temple Bar and its lively pubs and bars; it also has a wide selection of restaurants. For those who prefer a quieter evening away from the well-worn tourist track, there are plenty of sophisticated restaurants, trendy bars and low-key pubs.

> *'The most hospitable city I have ever passed through'*
>
> MARY WOLLSTONECRAFT
> *Letters* (1796)

———————•———————

The magnificent domed reading room at the National Library (right)

www.abbeytheatre.ie
- 29D4
- 26 Abbey Street Lower
- 878 7222
- Peformances Mon–Sat 8pm, Sat matinees 2:30; Peacock Theatre Mon–Sat 8:15pm, Sat matinees 2:45
- Tara Street, Connolly, Abbey LUAS
- Cross-city buses
- Abbey good; Peacock none
- Expensive, varies according to performance
- Backstage tours on Thu 887 7223
- Custom House (➤ 40), General Post Office (➤ 18)

ABBEY THEATRE

The Irish National Theatre was founded in 1903 by co-directors W B Yeats and Lady Augusta Gregory. Premises were purchased in Abbey Street and the new theatre was first opened to the public on 27 December, 1904. In its early days there were riots after performances of plays by playwrights such as Sean O'Casey. Following a fire in 1951, the Abbey remained closed until 1966. The Peacock Theatre was incorporated in the basement with the prime object of showcasing new plays by burgeoning Irish writers. Established writers, including Brian Friel and Hugh Leonard, have their new works premièred here, and classic plays, such as *The Playboy of the Western* World by J M Synge, are regularly produced.

The Abbey Theatre, where many an Irish writer has staged their play

BALLSBRIDGE

This leafy suburb was laid out mainly in the mid-19th century but it still retains some grand Georgian houses making it an exclusive and expensive place to live. It is sometimes known as the Embassy district, as foreign consulates have established themselves here, along with smart upmarket hotels and the Royal Dublin Society Showgrounds, where prestigious events are held, such as the Dublin Horse Show. Close to the Lansdowne Road DART station is the famous Irish national rugby stadium, another Ballsbridge landmark.

- Off map at 29F1
- Southeast of city centre
- Lansdowne Road
- 5, 7, 7A, 18, 45, 46, 84

BANK OF IRELAND

The bank began life as the upper and lower houses of the old Irish Parliament in 1739, the first purpose-built parliament buildings in Europe. The House of Commons was destroyed by fire in 1792, but the House of Lords remains intact and can be visited. The Act of Union of 1800 shifted direct rule to London and the parliament buildings, on becoming redundant, were purchased by the Bank of Ireland in 1802. The House of Lords has a fine vaulted ceiling and oak panelling, a sparkling Waterford crystal chandelier and huge tapestries depicting the 1689 siege at Londonderry and the 1690 battle of the Boyne.

- 29D3
- 2 College Green
- 677 6801
- House of Lords: Mon, Tue, Fri 10–4, Wed 10:30–4, Thu 10–5. Bank of Ireland Arts Centre: Tue–Fri 10–4
- Tara Street
- Cross-city buses
- Few
- Free; arts centre inexpensive

Going through the Foster Place entrance you can visit the Bank of Ireland Arts Centre, which features an exhibition, the 'Story of Banking'. The mace, made in 1765, was retained despite the British Government's insistence that all traces of the Irish House of Commons were removed. The centre also hosts lunchtime concerts and a range of evening cultural events.

BEWLEY'S ORIENTAL CAFÉS ✪✪

These cafés are a Dublin institution and the premises at Grafton Street and Westmoreland Street are well worth visiting for the ambience alone. The family connection goes back to the 1840s when Joshua Bewley set up as a tea merchant. His son Ernest opened the first branch in South Great St Georges Street (now closed) in 1894, followed by the Westmoreland branch in 1896. He introduced coffee and his wife baked scones and cakes. As the cafés grew in popularity, the family opened the now famous Grafton Street branch in 1927. Here you can sip coffee or eat a meal in the upstairs restaurant among the original art-nouveau and art-deco setting. This is where writers including Brendan Behan and Patrick Kavanagh came during the 1950s. On the first floor, in the former chocolate factory, there is a small museum displaying family portraits, old equipment and early teapots. The Bewley business has continued to expand, with further cafés in Waterstones bookshops and a contemporary café in Dublin airport.

- ✚ 29D3
- ✉ 78 Grafton Street; 10–12 Westmoreland Street
- ☎ 679 4085
- 🕐 Mon–Thu 7:30am–11pm, Fri–Sat 7:30am–1am, Sun 8am–11pm
- 🚆 Tara Street
- 🚌 Cross-city buses
- ♿ Ground floor good
- ↔ Trinity College (► 24–25), Bank of Ireland (► 32)

The history of the renowned Bewley's Cafés (above) dates back to the 19th century

The colonnaded exterior of the Bank of Ireland

BLESSINGTON STREET BASIN

Now known as Dublin's 'secret garden', Blessington is only 10 minutes' walk from O'Connell Street. The Basin was originally constructed around 1803 to provide a reservoir for the city's water supply. In the 1860s it was used exclusively to provide water to two distilleries – Jamesons in Bow Street and Powers in John's Lane – and this continued until the 1970s. The Basin was completely refurbished in 1994 and is now a peaceful haven for visitors and local residents, and a safe environment for wildlife.

BOOK OF KELLS (▶ 24–25, TOP TEN)

BOOTERSTOWN BIRD SANCTUARY

Booterstown Marsh is the only bird sanctuary in South Dublin Bay, an important feeding and roosting area for ducks, geese and waders. As part of the bay, Booterstown Marsh is an essential stop-over and refuelling place for migrating birds. There are both freshwater and saltwater habitats and the birds include moorhen, teal, snipe, oyster-catchers and Brent geese. During the 19th century most of the marsh was used for cultivation or grazing but has been drained subsequently and used for allotments. After World War II, when it fell into disuse, the marsh vegetation gradually reclaimed the arable land and now it is administered by the National Trust for Ireland; further development should include an interpretation centre and hide.

THE BRAM STOKER DRACULA EXPERIENCE

Bram Stoker, author of the famous novel *Dracula* (1897), was born in the seaside suburb of Clontarf. This museum, dedicated to him, opened in 2003 in a fitness club near the DART station, at a cost of over two million euros. It covers an area of 929sq m (10,000sq ft) and makes use of all the latest technology. The 'Time Tunnel to Transylvania', transports you to the depths of Count Dracula's castle, to the Blood Laboratory and Renfield's Lunatic Asylum; not for the faint-hearted. There is also a section devoted to Stoker's life and his literary achievements.

Left column listings:

✛ 28C5
✉ Blessington Street
☎ Dublin Parks 661 2369
◷ Dawn–Dusk
🚌 10A
♿ Good

✛ 77F3
✉ Booterstown, Co Dublin
☎ The National Trust for Ireland 454 1786
◷ Dawn–dusk
🚉 Booterstown
♿ Few

---

www.thebramstokerdraculaexperience.com
✛ 77F3
✉ Westwood Club, Clontarf Road
☎ 805 7824
◷ Fri–Sun noon–10
🍴 Restaurant, bar (€–€€)
🚉 Clontarf Road
🚌 27, 27B, 29A, 31, 32, 32A, 32B, 42, 42A, 42B, 43, 127, 129, 130
♿ Good

Blessington Street Basin: a calm and restful spot

34

A Stroll Along the Liffey Quays

Start from the magnificent Custom House (➤ 40) and follow along the quay west to O'Connell Bridge. After the bridge, stroll along the boardwalk by the side of the Liffey until you reach the Ha'penny Bridge (➤ 49), one of the oldest cast–iron structures of its kind in the world. Don't miss the sculpture known as 'the Hags with the Bags' here. Cross the bridge and turn right into Wellington Quay.

This quay was the last to be built, in 1812, and is lined with tall narrow merchants houses. Its most notable building is the Clarence Hotel (see page 100), converted from the 19th-century former Custom House and popular with celebrities.

Continue along the quay and glance left down Parliament Street where you can see the striking City Hall (➤ 36) built in 1769. On the other side of Parliament Street you pass the Sunlight Chambers (➤ 70). Look out for the attractive frieze on the building. You are now in Essex Quay.

Check out Betty Maguire's bronze *Viking Boat* sculpture. This was the area first settled by the Vikings in the 9th century.

Go past the Dublin Council offices on your left and head along Merchant's Quay. Glance across the water to the stunning Four Courts building (➤ 45), considered by many to be the finest public building in Dublin. Turn left into Bridge Street Lower. On your right is the Brazen Head.

This pub, the oldest in Dublin, has been trading for more than 800 years, although the current building dates from the 17th century.

Distance
1.5km (1 mile)

Time
1 hour

Start point
Custom House, Custom House Quay
✚ 29E4

End point
Brazen Head, 20 Bridge Street Lower
✚ 28B3

Lunch
Brazen Head (➤ 92)

Famine Figures at Custom House Quay commemorate the Great Famine of 1845–49

The south-facing façade of the Casino at Marino

📍 Off map at 29F5
✉ Off the Malahide Road, Marino
☎ 833 1618
🕐 Jun–Sep, daily 10–6; May, Oct,10–5; Apr, Sat–Sun noon–5; Feb, Mar, Nov, Dec, Sat–Sun noon–4. Last admission 50 minutes before closing
🍴 Clontarf Road
🚌 20A, 20B, 27, 27A, 27B, 42, 42C
♿ Few
💷 Inexpensive
❓ Visit by guided tour only

THE CASINO, MARINO ⭐⭐⭐

Although now surrounded by modern suburbia, the Casino ('small house') is one of the finest 18th-century neo-classical buildings in Ireland. George III's architect, Sir William Chambers, designed it along the lines of a Roman temple, and it contains 16 beautifully decorated rooms. It was built for James Caulfield, 1st Earl Charlemont, as a summer house where he could indulge his passion for all things Italian, following his Grand Tour of the Mediterranean. Throughout the rooms are fine ornamental plasterwork, exceptional parquet floors of rare woods, and practical features such as drainpipes hidden in ornate columns. The Casino was acquired by the state in 1930, after it had fallen into disrepair. Considerable restoration in the 1970s gradually returned it to its original condition, although work still continues.

CHRIST CHURCH CATHEDRAL (▶ 16, TOP TEN)

CITY HALL ⭐

www.dublincity.ie/cityhall
📍 28C3
✉ Cork Hill, Dame Street
☎ 672 2204
🕐 Mon–Sat 10–5:15, Sun & public hols 2–5
🚌 Cross-city buses
♿ Good
💷 Moderate
❓ Dublin Castle (▶ 17)

This imposing building, with its striking Corinthian portico, was originally designed by Thomas Cooley between 1769 and 1779 to house the Royal Exchange, and became the headquarters of the Dublin Corporation in 1852. In 2000 the interior of the building was restored to its former Georgian magnificence. It's worth going inside just to admire its superb rotunda, stunningly lit by the huge windows. In the vaulted basement the multimedia exhibition 'The Story of the Capital' tells the story of Dublin from its beginnings to the present day, with special attention to the development of civic government. There are displays of civic regalia, including the Great City Sword and the Great Mace. You can trace the history of Dublin through invasion, rebellion, civil war and plague, and the impact of the Viking, Norman, French-Huguenot and British rule on the city.

COLLINS BARRACKS ✪✪✪

One of the most impressive museum spaces in Europe, the former barracks now houses the National Museum of Decorative Arts & History and is the administrative headquarters of the National Museum of Ireland. It was built as the Royal Barracks in 1704 by Sir Thomas Burgh; it could accommodate 5,000 troops and was renamed Collins Barracks in memory of Republican hero Michael Collins, following Irish independence. In 1994 the barracks were assigned to the National Museum of Ireland and after extensive restoration they now display some of the 250,000 artefacts that make up exhibits charting Ireland's economic, social, political and military progress. There is an awesome collection of silver, ceramics, glassware, weapons, furniture and costume. Highlights include the rare 14th-century Fonthill Vase, 19th-century neo-Celtic furniture and costume and jewellery in 'The Way we Wore' exhibition. Don't miss the 'Curator's Choice' – 25 objects especially chosen by the curators of the various collections. Further developments will include more temporary exhibition space and galleries to accommodate ethnography and earth sciences displays.

www.museum.ie
- 🔲 28A4
- ✉ Benburb Street
- ☎ 677 7444
- 🕐 Tue–Sat 10–5, Sun 2–5
- 🍴 Museum café (€)
- 🚊 Heuston LUAS
- 🚌 25, 25A, 66, 67, 90
- ♿ Very good
- 💷 Free; guided tours inexpensive

The Drummond Memorial (left) stands in the entrance hall of Dublin's City Hall.
Imposing exterior of Collins Barracks (below)

In the Know

If you only have a short time to visit Dublin, or would like to get a real flavour of the city, here are some ideas:

10
Ways To Be A Local

Relax and take things slow – the local saying is: God created time then he gave the Irish more of it.

Listen to traditional music. Most Dubliners have been brought up on it and you'll find free performances in many city pubs.

Acquire a taste for Guinness. You cannot avoid it with so many tempting pubs, but be patient – the secret is to let it settle.

Go to a match. Join the crowds at Croke Park to watch some exciting hurling (similar to field hockey) or Gaelic football (a soccer-rugby hybrid).

Take up golf – a Dubliner's favourite pastime. There are plenty of courses to try.

Take the weather in your stride. The chances of rain are high. Shelter in a cosy café and wait for it to stop.

Relax in a park. It's not just tourists who seek refuge in a park and there are plenty to choose from in and around the city.

Party with the young. Dublin has the youngest population in Europe, so let your hair down, get out there and join in the fun.

Don't take life too seriously – the Irish are renowned for their sense of humour.

Stop for a chat and don't be frightened to start a conversation; many Irish people love to talk.

10
Good Places To Have Lunch

Avoca (€)
A popular spot for wholesome home-made food or a light salad. Scrumptious desserts and good coffee. On the top floor of the Avoca department store.
✉ 11–13 Suffolk Street
☎ 677 4215

Bad Ass Café (€)
Drop in for a burger or pizza at this well-known, unpretentious café in Temple Bar that has been appealing to young Dubliners for over 20 years. ✉ 9–11 Crown Alley ☎ 671 2596

Bewley's Oriental Café (€–€€)
You can't visit Dublin without taking a break in the legendary surroundings of Bewley's. ✉ 78–79 Grafton Street ☎ 635 5470

Brazen Head (€€)
Traditional old-world pub where the lunch-time carvery is a tempting option. ✉ 20 Bridge Street Lower ☎ 679 5186

Café Mao (€€)
Try the delicious stir-fries at this lively restaurant serving the best in Asian food. ✉ 2–3 Chatham Row ☎ 670 4899

Eden (€€€)
Pristine restaurant overlooking busy Meeting House Square in Temple Bar, serving excellent modern Irish cuisine.
✉ Meeting House Square
☎ 670 5372

Guinea Pig Fish Restaurant (€€€)
If you want to get out of town and sample the freshest fish, try this family-run seaside establishment.
✉ 17 Railway Road, Dalkey ☎ 285 9055

Leo Burdock's (€)
If you haven't the time or inclination to eat in, this classic take-away fish-and-chip shop has been frying since 1913.
✉ 2 Werburgh Street
☎ 454 0306

Nude (€)
Help do your bit for the environment at this eco-friendly eatery, which serves healthy options.
✉ 21 Suffolk Street
☎ 677 4804

Sign for the traditional Brazen Head pub, Dublin

Queen of Tarts (€)
Enjoy excellent home cooking here, including mouth-watering sweet and savoury pastries and great sandwiches. ⊠ 4 Cork Hill, Dame Street ☎ 670 7499

10
Best Statues/ Sculptures

A bronze of James Joyce in casual pose, complete with obligatory hat and walking stick, can be found at the end of Earl Street.
The Children of Lír in the Garden of Remembrance. Oisín Kelly's bronze dedicated to those who died in the pursuit of Irish independence.
Daniel O'Connell dominates the end of O'Connell Street, near the bridge, where this imposing monument was erected in 1882.
Famine Figures on the Custom House Quay commemorate the suffering of the Great Famine of 1845–49.
The Fusiliers' Arch at the entrance to St Stephen's Green is a tribute to the Royal Dublin Fusiliers lost in the Boer War.
Meeting Place by Jakki Mckenna, next to the Ha'Penny Bridge, is known locally as 'The Hags with the Bags'.
Molly Malone or the 'Tart with the Cart' still plies her cockles and mussels in Lower Grafton Street.
Oscar Wilde reclines languorously on a rock in Merrion Square, close to the house he lived in from 1855 to 1876.
Patrick Kavanagh, the poet, sits in meditation on a bench by the leafy Grand Canal.
The Viking Boat on Essex Quay by Betty Maguire reflects on the city's Viking origins.

10
Best Pubs

The Brazen Head is said to be the oldest pub in Dublin, trading for some 800 years. ⊠ 20 Bridge Street Lower ☎ 679 5186
Davy Byrnes has strong literary connections with James Joyce. ⊠ 21 Duke Street ☎ 677 5217
Doheny & Nesbitt is a glorious old pub frequented by politicians and journalists. ⊠ 5 Lower Baggot Street ☎ 676 2945
The Long Hall, where time has stood still, is ornately Victorian and has an exceptionally long bar. ⊠ 51 South Great George's Street ☎ 475 1590
McDaid's, once a morgue and a Moravian chapel, was popular with literary giants – Brendan Behan and friends drank here. ⊠ 3 Harry Street ☎ 679 4395
Messrs Maguire in the former library on three floors has its own microbrewery. Good food too. ⊠ 1–2 Burgh Quay ☎ 670 5777
Mulligan's, established in 1782, serves one of the

Irish music at the Oliver St John Gogarty pub

best pints of Guinness in the city. ⊠ 8 Poolbeg Street ☎ 677 5582
O'Donoghue's has been entertaining generations of Dubliners with its traditional music and great *craic*. ⊠ 15 Merrion Row ☎ 660 7194
Oliver St John Gogarty in Temple Bar is popular with tourists but it still retains its traditional ambience with Irish music and good local food. ⊠ 58–59 Fleet Street ☎ 671 1822
The Stag's Head in the heart of Georgian Dublin has wonderful period features. ⊠ 1 Dame Court ☎ 679 3701

5
Best Views

The Gravity Bar, Guinness Storehouse (➤ 19).
The Chimney at Smithfield (➤ 110).
St Michael's tower, Dvblinia (➤ 44).
Howth Head, Howth (➤ 52).
James Joyce Tower, Sandycove (➤ 68).

5
Places to See and Be Seen

Clarence Hotel (➤ 100).
Café en Seine (➤ 114).
Lillie's Bordello (➤ 113).
Patrick Guilbaud (➤ 96).
Shelbourne (➤ 101).

CUSTOM HOUSE

The best view of this impressive Georgian building, just past Eden Quay, is from the south side of the River Liffey. The huge neo-classical Custom House – 114m (375ft) long – was designed by James Gandon in 1791 as the port of Dublin became increasingly more important to the city. The Act of Union of 1800 put paid to this as the custom and excise business moved to London and its role became redundant. Stretching along the waterfront, the main façade is made up of arched arcades with a Doric portico at its centre. It is topped by a green copper cupola or dome 38m (125ft) high with a 5m (16ft) statue of Commerce crowning the dome. Look for the frieze above the centre for a series of 14 allegorical heads that represent the 13 rivers of Ireland and the Atlantic Ocean. Other statues represent the four continents, while those of cattle emphasize Dublin's beef trade. The building suffered fire damage during one of the more dramatic events of 1921, although it was not completely destroyed, and restoration took place after the fire and again in the 1980s. The building now contains government offices and a Visitor Centre complete with its Gandon Museum and a history of the Custom House.

DALKEY

Just a few stops on the DART south of the city is the pretty seaside village of Dalkey, once called the 'town of seven castles'. Only two of these fortified houses now remain, standing opposite each other in the attractive main street. Goat Castle remains totally intact and houses the **Heritage Centre**, with displays on the once important port. The view of the sea and mountains from the battlements is splendid. There are some good pubs and restaurants, and in summer you can visit Dalkey Island by boat, just a short distance offshore.

29E4
Custom House Quay
888 2538
Mid-Mar to Nov, Mon–Fri 10–12:30, Sat–Sun 2–5; Nov to mid-Mar, Wed–Fri 10–12:30, Sun 2–5
Tara Street
Cross-city buses
Good (Mon–Fri)
Inexpensive

Spectacular view of the Custom House, reflected in the River Liffey, at dusk (above)

77F3
Dalkey

Dalkey Castle & Heritage Centre
www.dalkeycastle.com
Castle Street, Dalkey
285 8366
Mon–Fri 9:30–5, Sat–Sun & public hols 11–5
Few
moderate

DART ⭐⭐

The Dublin Light Railway Transit or DART is an electrified train service that started in 1984, carrying some 35,000 travellers a day. At present around 80,000 people use the service daily and 26 more distinctive green carriages have now been added to the original 80. The transit line hugs Dublin Bay for 40km (25 miles) to the north of the city as far as Howth and Malahide and to the south down to Greystones. There are two major city-centre stations, Pearse and Connolly; Grand Canal Dock was the latest station to open in 2001. A trip on the DART is an ideal way of visiting the outlying districts of Dublin with excellent coastal views on the way.

- www.irishrail.ie
- ☎ 836 6222
- ◷ Trains run Mon–Sat 6:30am–11:30pm, Sun 9:30am–11pm; every 5 minutes at peak times, otherwise every 15 minutes and less frequently on Sun
- ♿ Contact in advance
- ❓ Until April 2005 the DART (northbound from Tara Street) will close at weekends for maintenance

DOLLYMOUNT STRAND ⭐

Only 20 minutes from the city centre, Dollymount Strand is a 3km (2-mile) long beach, a perfect place for walking, paddling or flying a kite. Nearby North Bull Island, a 300ha island formed after the construction of the Bull Wall (a North Sea wall) in the 1820s, is an important nature reserve and bird sanctuary with some 25,000 wading birds visiting in winter. You can drive on to the expanse of sand via a bridge at the west end and a causeway in the middle. A visitor centre opens in summer (daily 10–4:30) to help with the identification of wildlife. There are splendid views across the bay to the Wicklow Mountains.

- ✚ 77F3
- ✉ North Bull Island, Causeway Road, off James Larking Road
- 🚆 Clontarf Road 20 minutes
- 🚌 130
- ♿ Good; you can drive on to beach
- ✋ Free

DRIMNAGH CASTLE ⭐

You need to search for this one as it's hidden behind school buildings in the western outskirts of Dublin. But it's worth the effort as this is an outstanding example of an old feudal stronghold. Until 1954 it was one of the oldest continually inhabited castles in Ireland. The only Irish castle to have a full moat, it is set in a wonderfully restored 17th-century garden. From the 1950s the castle was in a bad state of repair and was not restored until the 1980s, when traditional craft skills were used to return it to its former glory. You can view the Great Hall, medieval undercroft and the tall tower with lookout posts.

- ✚ Off map at 28A3
- ✉ Long Mile Road, Drimnagh
- ☎ 450 2530
- ◷ Wed, noon–5, Sun, 2–5 or by appointment
- 🍴 Tea room (€)
- 🚆 Drimnagh LUAS
- 🚌 77, 77A, 56, 18
- ♿ Gardens good; castle none
- ✋ Moderate
- 🛍 Shop

DID YOU KNOW?

A series of life-sized, emaciated bronze figures along the quay in front of the Custom House commemorate the Great Famine of 1845–49. These reminders of Ireland's struggle in the 19th century, known as the *Famine Figures*, were sculpted by Rowan Gillespie in 1997.

DUBLIN CASTLE & CHESTER BEATTY LIBRARY (▶ 17, TOP TEN)

DUBLIN CITY LIBRARY & ARCHIVE

www.iol.ie/dublincitylibrary
➕ 29E3
✉ 138–144 Pearse Street
☎ 674 4800
🕐 Mon–Thu 10–8, Fri–Sat 10–5
🚉 Pearse
🚌 2, 3
♿ Good
✋ Free

The library, re-opened in July 2003 after major refurbishment, offers all the usual facilities of a lending library, plus a business information facility and music library. Of most interest to visitors are the excellent Dublin City Archive and Dublin & Irish Local Studies Collections. These archives contain the records of Dublin's civic government since 1171 and give a vivid picture of the city over eight centuries. In the local studies section there is a fascinating collection of books, newspapers, photographs, maps, prints, theatre programmes, posters, ballad sheets and audio-visual material giving a unique insight into the city of Dublin. You can look through the local parish records and trace your family history if you have Irish ancestors, although the main centre of genealogical studies is at the National Library (▶ 59) in Kildare Street. There is also a 100-seat Public Reading room and a café.

DUBLIN WRITERS MUSEUM

➕ 28C5
✉ 18 Parnell Square North
☎ 872 2077
🕐 Jun–Aug, Mon–Fri 10–6, Sat 10–5, Sun 11–5; Sep–May, Mon–Sat 10–5, Sun and public hols 11–5
🍴 Chapter One restaurant (€€; closed Sun–Mon) and café (€; closed Sun & public hols)
🚉 Connolly
🚌 Cross-city buses
♿ Good
✋ Expensive
❓ Self-guided audio tour (30 minutes); combined ticket available with James Joyce Museum (▶ 68) and Shaw's Birthplace (▶ 69)

The need to highlight the Irish literary tradition and the important place Dublin holds in the history of literature became apparent to the journalist and author Maurice Gorham (1902–75), who was the first to propose the idea of this museum to Dublin Tourism. It was not, however, until 1991 that the museum finally came to fruition. Ireland has produced a staggering number of the world's greatest writers and where better to showcase their work than in this glorious 18th-century town house in central Dublin. The aim of the museum is to promote interest in Irish literature and through its association with the Irish Writers'

Opulent decor in the Writer's Gallery at the Dublin Writers Museum

Centre, next door, to encourage today's writers. The town house accommodates the museum rooms, library, gallery and offices, while an annexe behind houses the coffee shop, bookshop, and exhibition and lecture rooms. The basement is home to the Chapter One restaurant (► 93).

Take advantage of the audio commentary that leads you through the displays, giving you the background story to Dublin's literary heritage. All the best-known Irish writers are represented, including Jonathan Swift, Oscar Wilde, George Bernard Shaw, Bram Stoker, James Joyce, W B Yeats, Samuel Beckett and Brendan Behan. Displays include letters, manuscripts, paintings and personal belongings and memorabilia. A highlight is Oliver St John Gogarty's flying goggles, hardly a literary artefact, but such items help to provide an intimate insight into the life of an author. The museum also has a room devoted to children's literature, and hosts regular readings and temporary exhibitions. Take a little time to view the building itself, with its exceptional stucco plasterwork and sumptuous furnishings.

DUBLIN ZOO ✪✪✪

Set in a beautifully landscaped area of Phoenix Park, Dublin Zoo covers some 26ha. It was founded in 1830 with animals supplied by London Zoo and is now one of the top attractions in Ireland. The aim of the zoo has changed since its early days, when the prime objective was to show people, who had never seen the like before, as many different species as possible. Today the zoo is concerned with conservation, education and animal study and it is part of an important international programme to breed and preserve endangered species, in particular the golden lion tamarin and the Moluccan cockatoo. One of

the recent additions has been the creation of the African Plains, consisting of a large lake, pasture land and mature woodland. The animals featured on the plain include giraffes, hippos, rhinos, chimpanzees, lions, cheetahs and ostriches. Here they can wander freely within large fenced paddocks, with access to pools and trees. Take the Nakuru Safari, a 25-minute tour of the African Plains, with full on-board commentary. Other highlights are the World of Cats, the Fringes of the Arctic and the City Farm, where children can handle pet and farm animals.

www.dublinzoo.ie
* Off map at 28A3
* Phoenix Park
* 677 1425
* Mar–Sep, Mon–Sat 9:30–6, Sun 10:30–6; Oct–Feb, Mon–Sat 9:30–dusk, Sun 10:30–dusk. Last admission one hour before closing. Nakuru Safari daily between 11 and 4
* Restaurant, cafés (€), picnic areas
* Heuston LUAS
* 10, 10A, 25, 26, 66, 66A, 66B, 67, 67A
* Good
* Expensive; Nakuru Safari extra, moderate

77F3

Dun Laoghaire

7, 7A, 46A, 746

National Maritime Museum

High Terrace, Dun
Laoghaire

280 0969

May–Sep, Tue–Sun 1–5

DUN LAOGHAIRE AND THE NATIONAL MARITIME MUSEUM

Dun Laoghaire (pronounced 'Dun Leary') boasts a fine harbour and is well known both as a seaside resort and a thriving port where car ferries from Holyhead on the Isle of Anglesey in Wales dock. From a small fishing village in the early 19th century, the town is now a thriving community and a popular venue for the people of Dublin to visit at weekends. There's plenty to do, with lots of pubs and restaurants, watersports, boat trips around the bay and fishing, plus excellent walking and views along the coast. The **National Maritime Museum** in the Mariner's Church has displays of model boats and Irish naval memorabilia. Take a look at the Bantry boat, a 12m (40ft) French longboat captured during the failed French invasion of 1796; it remains in excellent condition.

DVBLINIA

This award-winning exhibition reproduces the sights and sounds of medieval Dublin. It is housed in the former Synod Hall and is joined to Christ Church Cathedral by a bridge. Note that the bridge is only one way – into the cathedral – so visit Dvblinia first. The exhibition gives you the chance to experience medieval life at first-hand through reconstructions of life-sized streets and houses. Major events in Dublin's history are re-created, including the Black Death and early rebellion. There are also artefacts removed from the excavation of nearby Wood Quay, which revealed Norse and Viking items such as pottery, coins and swords. From the top of the 60m (197ft) St Michael's Tower you can enjoy great views of the city.

www.dublinia.ie

28B3

St Michael's Hill,
Christchurch

679 4611

Apr–Sep, daily 10–5;
Oct–Mar, Mon–Sat 11–4,
Sun & public hols
10–4:30

Tea room Jun–Aug (€)

Cross-city buses

Good; no access to
Tower

Moderate (including
Christ Church)

Christ Church Cathedral
(► 16)

*Small boats bobbing on
the water in Dun
Laoghaire harbour*

FITZWILLIAM SQUARE ✪✪

This is one of Dublin's most famous squares and the last to be completed, in 1825. The first house was built here in 1714, which means the square's architecture spans the reigns of all four Georgian kings. The central garden is private and only the residents hold keys. The artist Jack B Yeats (1871–1957), who lived at No 18, is among some of the illustrious people to have resided here. There is plenty

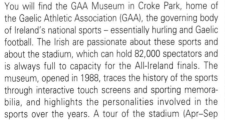

of Georgian detail, including original fanlights, and on some houses a box-shaped recess that held the lamps. Look, too, for original door knockers and elaborate iron foot-scrapers. Some houses have spikes set into the wall beside the windows to deter 19th-century burglars, and there are examples of ornamental iron balconies and attractive metal coal-hole covers.

🔲 29E1
🚌 Cross-city buses
✋ Free

An elegant ivy-clad Georgian front door

FOUR COURTS ✪

Four Courts was built by James Gandon between 1786 and 1802. This huge Georgian complex along the river is still Ireland's main criminal court so you can visit only when court is in session, although you cannot enter the courts and restricted areas. The building suffered heavy damage during the Civil War and was not restored until the 1930s. There are some fine statues on the six-columned portico.

🔲 28B3
✉ Inns Quay
🚊 Four Courts LUAS
☎ 872 5555
🕐 Mon–Fri 10–1, 2–4 only when court is in session
🚌 Cross-city buses
♿ Few
✋ Free

GAA MUSEUM ✪

You will find the GAA Museum in Croke Park, home of the Gaelic Athletic Association (GAA), the governing body of Ireland's national sports – essentially hurling and Gaelic football. The Irish are passionate about these sports and about the stadium, which can hold 82,000 spectators and is always full to capacity for the All-Ireland finals. The museum, opened in 1988, traces the history of the sports through interactive touch screens and sporting memorabilia, and highlights the personalities involved in the sports over the years. A tour of the stadium (Apr–Sep 12:30 and 3pm; Oct–Mar 2pm) includes a look behind the scenes as well as an opportunity to see the pitch.

www.gaa.ie
🔲 Off map at 29D5
✉ Croke Park, St Joseph's Avenue
☎ 819 2323
🕐 Mon–Sat 9:30–5, Sun & public hols noon–5 (not open on match days)
🍴 Coffee shop (€)
🚆 Connolly (15-minute walk)
🚌 3, 11, 11A, 16, 16A
♿ Good
✋ Moderate–expensive

45

A Walk in the Footsteps of Joyce

Distance
2km (1.2 miles)

Time
1 hour 30 minutes, more including stops

Start point
James Joyce Cultural Centre, 35 North Great George Street
✚ 29D5

End point
National Museum, Kildare Street
✚ 29E2

Lunch
National Museum café, Kildare Street (€)
☎ 677 7444

From the James Joyce Cultural Centre (➤ 20) in North Great George Street walk down the street and cross over Parnell Street into Marlborough Street. Go past St Mary's Pro-Cathedral on the right. Take the second right into Earl Street North, where you will find a statue of Joyce. Turn left into O'Connell Street. Cross over, and as you pass the GPO building (➤ 18) take the second right into Abbey Street.

Outside Eason's bookshop (No 78–79) you will find the first of 14 bronze plaques in the pavement, marking the route taken by Leopold Bloom, hero of Joyce's novel *Ulysses*. Take time to read the quotes on the plaques.

James Joyce statue in Earl Street North

Retrace your steps to O'Connell Street and turn right; there's another plaque outside No 49. Continue over the bridge.

On the corner of Aston Quay and Westmoreland Street is the Royal Liverpool Assurance building with a plaque outside.

Cross over Westmoreland Street. On the left at No 29, formerly Harrison's bakery, is another plaque. Continue until you come to the traffic island with a statue of Thomas More and a further plaque. Continue with Trinity College to your left, up Grafton Street and take the third left into Duke Street.

On the right is David Byrne's pub, a haunt of both Joyce and his fictional hero Bloom.

Continue and turn right at the end into Dawson Street, taking the next left into Molesworth Street. Look out for a plaque on the left. Cross into Kildare Street and the final plaque is across the road outside the old entrance to the National Museum (➤ 23).

GATE THEATRE ✪

Established in 1928, the Gate is housed in an elegant late-Georgian building, originally the grand supper room of the Rotunda in Parnell Square. From the outset the Gate offered Dublin audiences the best of international productions, as well as plays from the classic and contemporary Irish repertoire. Many famous names first performed at the Gate, including James Mason and a young Orson Welles. The Gate also presents festivals of works by playwrights such as Harold Pinter and Samuel Beckett and has special relationships with many well-known Irish writers, including Brian Friel and Frank McGuinness. Check the website for latest productions.

www.gate-theatre.ie
🔲 29D5
✉ 1 Cavendish Row, Parnell Square East
☎ 874 4085, box office 874 4045
🕐 Check for performance times, building open Mon–Sat 10–7
🚌 Cross-city buses
♿ Good
✋ Depends on performance

Glasnevin Cemetery (below)

GLASNEVIN CEMETERY ✪✪✪

This cemetery, originally known as Prospect Cemetery, was established in 1832 by Daniel O'Connell (➤ 14) when Catholics were at last legally allowed to conduct funerals. It is Ireland's largest cemetery, set in 49ha (121 acres) of landscaped grounds, and around 1.2 million people are buried here. Here you will find ornately carved Celtic crosses, Gothic mausoleums and tombs of the famous. Join one of the free tours to discover the dazzling array of well-known Irish people who have been buried here in the

www.glasnevin-cemetry.ie
🔲 Off map at 28B5
✉ Finglas Road, Glasnevin
☎ 830 1133
🕐 Mon–Sat 8:30–4:30, Sun 9–4:30
🚌 19, 40
♿ Good; except to crypt
💶 Free
❓ Tours Wed, Fri 2:30; approx 2 hours

last two centuries. The names are synonymous with Dublin and Ireland, both political and cultural. Charles Stewart Parnell, Michael Collins and Eamon de Valera – the latter a leader of the 1916 Easter Rising, who went on to be Taoiseach seven times and President of Ireland twice – are among the famous political names. W B Yeats, Brendan Behan, the poet Gerald Manley Hopkins and the arts benefactor Alfred Chester Beatty lie here too. There are plenty of controversial names reflecting Ireland's turbulent past; of particular note is Sir Roger Casement, who was executed by the British for treason in 1916 and whose remains were kept in London until 1964. O'Connell is commemorated by a 51m (167ft) tall round tower. Famous names aside, the pauper's graves are poignant reminders of the devastation wrought by famine and cholera in the 1840s.

GENERAL POST OFFICE (▶ 18, TOP TEN)

GRAFTON STREET ⊕⊕

29D3
Grafton Street
Tara Street/Pearse
Cross-city buses

Dublin's most popular thoroughfare is only 200m (650ft) long and 6m (20ft) wide and at times it gets full to bursting. This attractive pedestrianized street, linking Trinity College and St Stephen's Green, is lined with four-storey Georgian buildings, and together with some of the smaller alleyways off the street, houses a selection of Dublin's best shops, restaurants, cafés – especially Bewleys (▶ 33) – pubs and bars. Flower sellers and street musicians add to this attractive city scene.

GRAND CANAL ⊕

29F2
Grand Canal Quay
Grand Canal Dock
2, 3

Canals were the innovative form of cargo transport in the 18th century and Dublin's Grand Canal and Royal Canal were no exception. The Grand Canal crossed Leinster from Dublin to the River Shannon in Offaly, with a branch south

to join the lovely River Barrow. Some 6km (3.8 miles) of the canal loop around Dublin. though it has carried no commercial traffic since the early 1960s. It's a pleasant place to stroll or take a boat trip, and is a haven for wildlife. At Grand Canal Quay, a few minutes' walk from the DART city station, is the Waterways Island Visitor Centre (▶ 73), which houses an interactive multimedia exhibition of Ireland's inland waterways. It forms part of the quay's ambitious development project, which will include a new marina, apartments and offices. A good two-hour walk along the towpath takes you all the way to Kilmainham. You can rest on the bench near Baggot Street Bridge, next to the bronze statue of poet Patrick Kavanagh (1905–67), who loved this stretch of water.

Brown Thomas department store on Grafton Street (above)

People crossing the Ha'penny Bridge (right)

An intricately decorated coat on display in the Heraldic Museum

GUINNESS STOREHOUSE (▶ 19, TOP TEN)

HA'PENNY BRIDGE ⭐⭐

This central Dublin landmark, originally called the Wellington Bridge after the Duke of Wellington, opened in 1816. It gained its nickname because up until 1919 it cost one old half penny to go over the bridge. Before the opening of the new Millennium Bridge in 2000 it was the only pedestrian bridge across the Liffey. Cast at Coalbrookdale in Shropshire, England, the ornate, arched footbridge was renovated in 2001 and repainted its historically correct off-white. Three lamps supported by carved ironwork span the walkway which, together with the old-fashioned lampposts at either end, make the bridge particularly attractive when illuminated at night.

🔶 29D3
✉ Between Liffey Street Lower (north side) and Crown Alley (south side)
🚇 Tara Street
🚌 Cross-city buses

HERALDIC MUSEUM ⭐⭐

The Heraldic Museum has been attached to the Office of the Chief Herald since 1909 and is an integral part of the National Library. It is housed in an attractive 19th-century building, the former Kildare Street Club, designed by Benjamin Woodward. Attractive carvings on the exterior include monkeys playing billiards and decorative birds. In the main exhibition room you can see the modern banners of Ireland's ancient chieftain families, creating a colourful display, along with paintings, Belleek pottery and shields. Note the colours of the Irish infantry regiments who fought in France during the 18th century. From further afield are the arms of Napoleon, Sir Francis Drake and the Spencer-Churchill family. The museum also traces the origins of heraldry both in Ireland and throughout Europe.

🔶 29E2
✉ 2 Kildare Street
☎ 603 0311
🕐 Mon–Wed 10–8, Thu–Fri 10–4:30, Sat 10–12:30
🚇 Pearse
🚌 Cross-city buses
♿ None
🎫 Free
↔ National Library (▶ 59), National Gallery (▶ 22), National Museum (▶ 23)

Food & Drink

The choice of places to eat out in Dublin is excellent and the standard of many restaurants is first class. There is a strong emphasis on global cuisine, with options as diverse as Mongolian, Lebanese, Mexican and Nepalese. A host of talented Irish chefs is now on the scene, ensuring good standards and the use of local ingredients.

Traditional Irish cuisine and good pub grub have enjoyed a revival, with the occasional international influence. Irish seafood is legendary, particularly fresh oysters, fresh and smoked salmon and the well-known Dublin Bay prawns. Generally restaurants are not cheap, but there are plenty of good-value set meals available.

Irish Cuisine

Irish cooking has a reputation for being plain but plentiful, which is far from true – traditional dishes have wonderfully rich flavours and interesting taste combinations. The best chefs have moved away from the heavier dishes, which were mostly served to hard-working farmers and fishermen, and have created a new Irish cuisine, a fusion of flavours to produce a lighter result, but still reflecting the traditional theme. Some long-established choices remain, such as Dublin coddle (a sausage stew), but an alternative is to make it with shellfish, producing a lighter meal. Irish stew is still popular, as are potato dishes

Don't miss the chance to try some fresh fish (above) while in Dublin A typical selection of meats (right) in an Irish butcher's shop

such as champ (mashed with chives and butter) or colcannon (mashed and mixed with leek, butter, cabbage, cream and nutmeg), which are served as a tasty accompaniment. Boxties (potato pancakes with various savoury fillings) are served as a main course.

Irish bread is not just something to make a sandwich with. There are many tasty varieties that need only a spreading of butter or are used as a side dish for home-made soup. Soda bread, or wheaten bread, made with stone-ground flour, has a wonderful flavour and texture, then there are the fruity tea breads such as barm brack. There is even a potato bread (mashed potato mixed with flour and egg) that is cooked on a griddle and usually served with the hearty traditional Irish breakfast of bacon, eggs, sausage and black (or white) pudding.

What to Drink?

Think of Irish beer and Guinness springs to mind; it's been brewed in Dublin since 1799. Sold in at least 30 countries worldwide, it is an enduring symbol of Irishness, but undoubtedly tastes best on Irish soil, with its cool, biting flavour and thick creamy head. Lager is also widely available to those who prefer a lighter drink.

Irish whiskey has a wonderful clean taste, quite different from Scotch whisky or American bourbon. There are no longer any whiskey distilleries in Dublin, although Jameson's is still a household name; it was distilled in the city up until 1971. You can take a tour of The Old Jameson Distillery (➤ 63), which includes a free sample.

Symbolic of Dublin: A pint of Guinness (below). Pulling a pint of Guinness in the Doheny and Nesbitt pub in Lower Baggot Street (bottom)

🔲 77F3
⊠ Howth Head
🚉 Howth
🚌 31, 31B

National Transport Museum
www.
nationaltransportmuseum.org
⊠ Heritage Depot, Howth
Castle Demesne, Howth
☎ 848 0831
🕐 Jun–Aug, daily 10–5;
Sep–May, Sat–Sun &
public hols 2–5
♿ Few
💷 Inexpensive

HOWTH

A pleasant ride north on the DART will take you to Howth, a major fishing centre and yachting harbour. Howth (rhymes with both) is a popular residential suburb whose steep streets run down to the sea. The DART station is near the harbour and close to all the waterside activity, bars, pubs and restaurants. You can take a boat trip to view the small rocky island, Ireland's Eye, with its resident puffin colony, Martello tower and 6th-century monastic ruins. Above the town are the remains of St Mary's Abbey and 1km (0.6 mile) to the west is Howth Castle and the **National Transport Museum**. The 16th-century castle is closed to the public but the gardens are famous for their rhododendrons and azaleas. Hidden away in a farmyard is the transport museum, with its unique collection of restored old trams, fire engines and vans. From Howth Head there are splendid views over Dublin Bay, and an 8km (5-mile) waymarked path around the head makes a dramatic walk.

www.hughlane.ie
🔲 28C5
⊠ Charlemont House,
Parnell Square North
☎ 874 1903
🕐 Tue–Thu 9:30–6, Fri–Sat
9:30–5, Sun 11–5
🍴 Café (€)
🚉 Tara Street/Connolly
🚌 Cross-city buses
♿ Good
💷 Free; Bacon Studio
expensive
↔ Dublin Writers' Museum
(► 42–43)
❓ Guided tours by prior
arrangement

HUGH LANE GALLERY

Charlemont House in Parnell Square provides the perfect setting for the fine collection of modern art bequeathed to the nation by Sir Hugh Lane (1875–1915). There was controversy over part of the bequest as both London and Dublin laid claim to his legacy of Impressionist art. After much wrangling it was agreed that the paintings should be shared between both cities. Hugh Lane started his career as an apprentice art restorer and later became a successful London art dealer. He drowned when the *Lusitania* sank in 1915. The collection includes work by Monet, Degas and Renoir, as well as by 20th-century Irish artists such as Yeats and Orpen, and modern European artists including Beuys and Albers. You can also visit the re-created studio of the Dublin artist Francis Bacon here, with more than 7,500 items.

The Hugh Lane Gallery is home to a splendid collection of modern art

Around Dublin's Pubs

Begin at the Stag's Head (➤ 114) in Dame Court, a small road off Dame Lane. Walk south to Exchequer Street and turn left. Continue to the Old Stand, one of Dublin's oldest pubs, on the left. Opposite, on the corner of Wicklow Street, is the International Bar. Turn right into William Street South and leave Powerscourt Shopping Centre on your left; opposite is Grogan's.

A city-centre institution, Grogan's has long been popular with writers and artists.

Continue towards the end of the street, turning left into Chatham Row and into Chatham Street; Victorian-style Neary's is on your right. Turn left into Grafton Street and next left into Harry Street for McDaid's (➤ 114). Return to Grafton Street and go straight across to Anne Street South; halfway down is John Kehoe (➤ 114).

Kehoe's is an excellent example of a traditional old-style pub with plenty of *craic*.

Continue along Anne Street South and turn left into Dawson Street; take the next left into Duke Street to Davy Byrnes, a former haunt of James Joyce. Continue on and turn right into Grafton Street, then take the second left into Suffolk Street. Follow the road round into Church Lane where you will find O'Neill's, a popular student watering hole, on the corner. Follow the road round and turn left into Dame Street. Cross the road and take the first right into Anglesea Street. At the end is Oliver St John Gogarty (➤ 96) on the right and the Auld Dubliner on the left. Turn left into Temple Bar.

There are numerous pubs, bars and eating places here, including the Temple Bar (➤ 71) with its beer garden.

Distance
1.5km (1 mile)

Time
Depends how thirsty you are

Start point
Stag's Head, Dame Court
➕ 28C3

End point
The Temple Bar,
47–48 Temple Bar
➕ 29D3

Lunch
Good choice of pubs, restaurants and cafés in Temple Bar

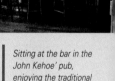

Sitting at the bar in the John Kehoe' pub, enjoying the traditional Irish atmosphere

➕ Off map at 28C1
✉ Walworth Road, off Victoria Street
☎ 453 1797
🕐 May–Sep, Tue, Thu, Sun 11–3:30; Oct–Apr, Sun 10:30–2:30
🚌 16, 16A 19, 19A
♿ Few
🎫 Free

Fountains at the Irish Museum of Modern Art

IRISH JEWISH MUSEUM ✪

The first Jewish people to settle in Ireland were from Portugal and Spain, fleeing persecution and the Inquisition. The former synagogue in which this museum is housed first opened in Dublin in 1918 and retains many of its original features. Opened in 1985 by Chaim Herzog, the Irish-born former president of Israel, the museum traces the history and the cultural, professional and commercial life of Dublin's small but active Jewish community. It also chronicles Jewish lives through paintings, books and photographs, and has a re-created kitchen scene showing a typical Sabbath meal from the early 1900s.

www.imma.ie
➕ Off map at 28A3
✉ Royal Hospital, Military Road, Kilmainham
☎ 612 9900
🕐 Tue–Sat 10–5:30, Sun & public hols noon–5:30
🍴 Café (€)
🚌 51B, 78A, 79, 90
♿ Good
🎫 Free; guided tours of the North Range: moderate
↔ Kilmainham Gaol (➤ 21)
❓ Formal gardens; bookshop

IRISH MUSEUM OF MODERN ART ✪✪

The magnificent Royal Hospital building that houses the Irish Museum of Modern Art was designed by Sir William Robinson in 1684 for the Duke of Ormonde as a home for retired soldiers and was based on Les Invalides in Paris. It

DID YOU KNOW?

The earliest reference to Jewish people in Ireland records the arrival of five Jews from 'over the sea' in 1079. It is believed that many more arrived after being expelled from Portugal at the end of the 15th century. The earliest recorded synagogue in Ireland dates from 1660; it was located in Crane Lane, opposite Dublin Castle. The oldest Jewish cemetery dates from the early 1700s and is situated in the Dublin suburb of Clontarf.

Relaxing in the pretty Iveagh Gardens

remained a home until 1927, and was finally restored in the 1980s. In 1991 it opened as the Irish Museum of Modern Art. Its stark grey-and-white interior provides a striking backdrop for the permanent collection of Irish and international modern and contemporary art. There are regular temporary exhibitions and a community programme covering music and the visual arts.

IVEAGH HOUSE AND GARDENS

Iveagh House was donated to the state by Sir Robert Guinness, 2nd Earl of Iveagh, in 1939. Originally two houses when built in the 1760s, the Guinness family bought the properties in the 1860s and linked them under a stone façade, incorporating the family arms on the pediment. They subsequently altered the interior to include a new ballroom with an impressive domed ceiling. The house is now used by the Department of Foreign Affairs but is not open to the public. Hidden beyond Iveagh House are the lovely, secluded Iveagh Gardens. This is one of Dublin's finest but least well known parks, just south of St Stephen's Green and entered by a small side street, Clonmel Street. Designed in 1863 by Ninian Niven, it includes a central area with lawns, statues and fountains echoing the Bois de Boulogne in Paris. Other areas have a more natural feel with a rustic grotto, woodlands and wilderness. There is also a maze and archery lawn reminiscent of Hampton Court in London. It's the perfect place to escape the hectic city on a warm summer's day.

JAMES JOYCE CULTURAL CENTRE (▶ 20, TOP TEN)

29D1
Clonmel Street
☎ 475 7816
Mar–Oct, Mon–Sat 8–6, Sun & public hols 10–6; Nov–Feb, Mon–Sat 8–4. Sun & public hols 10–4
Cross-city buses
Good; some steps
Free

A dramatic view from Dalkey Hill across Killiney Bay toward the distant Wicklow Hills

---

✚ 77F3
✉ Killiney
🚉 Killiney

KILLINEY   ★★

A short trip south on the DART takes you to the affluent village of Killiney, the 'Dublin Riviera', where national and international celebrities have set up home. But you don't have to be wealthy to enjoy some of the best views of Dublin and the surrounding area. The climb to the top of Killiney Hill takes about 30 minutes and rewards with exceptional vistas. Down at Coliemore Harbour fishermen run boat trips to nearby Dalkey Island, with its bird sanctuary, in summer.

KILMAINHAM GAOL (► 21, TOP TEN)

LEINSTER HOUSE   ★

This is one of Dublin's finest Georgian town houses; when it was built in 1745 for the Earl of Kildare it was the largest house of its type in Ireland. It was renamed when the Earl became Duke of Leinster in 1766. The building eventually passed to the government and from 1922, with the forming of the Irish Free State, it became the headquarters of the new government. Today Leinster House is the seat of the Oireachtas (parliament) and houses the Dáil (lower house) and the Seannad (upper house or Senate), and is only open to the public by guided tour when parliament is not sitting.

✚ 29E2
✉ Kildare Street
☎ 618 3166
🕐 Call for information
🍴 Café (€)
🚉 Pearse
🚌 Cross-city buses
♿ Good
💵 Free
❓ Visits, by tour only, take 2 hours

Malahide Castle features a variety of architectural styles

MALAHIDE ⭐⭐

Just 13km (8 miles) north of Dublin and easily reached by the DART is Malahide. This attractive seaside village has become an increasingly desirable place for Dubliners to live, and with its restaurants, pubs, chic shops and marina is popular with visitors too. One of the highlights on the edge of the village is **Malahide Castle**. Set in 100ha (247 acres) of woodland, the castle was both a fortress and a private home for nearly 800 years; the Talbot family lived here continuously from 1188 until 1973.

It is an interesting mix of architectural styles, with its central medieval core, a three-level, 12th-century tower, 16th-century oak room and additional Georgian embellishments and furnishings. You can see the Talbot family portraits, together with paintings loaned from the National Gallery, on organised tours. Keep an eye out for one of the many ghosts believed to haunt the castle. In a separate building in the grounds you will find the **Fry Model Railway Museum** (▶ 110), one of the world's largest collections of model railways.

➕ 77F3
🚇 Malahide
🚌 42

Malahide Castle
✉ Malahide Castle Demense, Malahide
☎ 846 2184
🕐 Apr–Oct, Mon–Sat 10–5, Sun & public hols 11–6; Nov–Mar, Mon–Sat 10–5, Sun & public hols 11–5
🍴 Restaurant (€€)
♿ None
💷 Expensive

MARSH'S LIBRARY ⭐⭐

This is the oldest public library in Ireland and has remained virtually unchanged throughout its 300-year history. It was built for Archbishop Narcissus Marsh to a design by Sir William Robinson, architect of the Royal Hospital at Kilmainham. There are some 25,000 volumes dating from the 15th to early 18th century, plus maps and manuscripts. The pervading atmosphere is one of learning and study, the books crammed high in the beautiful oak bookcases. At the far end of the reading gallery are three alcoves or 'cages' where scholars were locked in to avoid them

stealing the valuable tomes. Marsh's collection is wide ranging – the oldest book is Cicero's *Letters to his Friends*, published in 1472, and other highlights are signed copies of books by Jonathan Swift and English poet John Donne. Signatures in the guest book include those of James Joyce and Daniel O'Connell. If books are your passion, this library, at the very heart of literary Dublin, should not be missed.

www.marshlibrary.ie
➕ 28C2
✉ St Patrick's Close
☎ 454 3511
🕐 Mon, Wed, Thu, Fri 10–1, Sat 10:30–1
🚌 Cross-city buses
♿ Few; stairs to first floor
💷 Inexpensive
🔁 St Patrick's Cathedral (▶ 26)

A glimpse of the interior of Marsh's Library

✚ 29E2
✉ Merrion Square
🕐 Park: daylight hours only
🚉 Pearse
🚌 Cross-city buses

✚ Off map at 28B5
✉ Glasnevin
☎ 857 0909
🕐 Summer, Mon–Sat 9–6,
Sun 10–6; winter, daily
10–4. Glasshouses and
Alpine House restricted
hours
🚌 13, 19, 19A, 83
🚉 Drumcondra
♿ Good; some steep
gradients
💷 Free
↔ Glasnevin Cemetery
(➤ 47)
❓ Guided tours available by
prior arrangement
(inexpensive)

*An old-fashioned
lamppost in Merrion
Square (above)*

MERRION SQUARE ✪✪✪

Languishing on a rock on the edge of Merrion Square's central park is a superb statue of Oscar Wilde. The author lived at No 1 (➤ 64) between 1855 and 1876, and his house is a fine example of the city's Georgian architecture. Merrion is one of Dublin's most prestigious squares, laid out in 1762 by John Ensor, and bordered by Leinster House, the National Gallery, the Natural History Museum and numerous smaller examples of Georgian splendour. Here you will find town houses with wrought-iron balconies, brightly painted doors, fanlights and elaborate door-knockers. The learned and the illustrious have lived here, including W B Yeats and the Duke of Wellington. Just off the square is Number Twenty-Nine (➤ 63), a Georgian gem. The park is a delightful place to be on a sunny day, with its outstanding array of seasonal floral displays. Every Saturday and Sunday (10–6:30) there is an art display in the park, where over a hundred artists exhibit and sell their own art work.

NATIONAL BOTANIC GARDENS

To the north of the city, near Glasnevin Cemetery, are thees botanic gardens, which opened in 1795. Apart from being a delightful place to stroll, they are also Ireland's premier centre for botany and horticulture. The heart of the gardens are the beautifully-restored Victorian glass and cast-iron curvilinear buildings, including the Palm House. These glasshouses contain plants from across the world, including bamboo, banana and orchids. Outside, there is a rare handkerchief tree from China. In the Aquatic House you will find a variety of spectacular Amazonian water lilies. The 20ha (50-acre) park has around 20,000 different species of flora. Particular highlights include an arboretum, rock garden and Burren area, rose gardens, yew tree walk, the glorious herbaceous borders and a rare example of Victorian carpet bedding. An education and visitor centre opened in 2000 to give people further insight into the work of the botanic gardens.

NATIONAL GALLERY (➤ 22, TOP TEN)

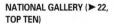

NATIONAL LIBRARY ⭐

The library opened in 1890 in a late 19th-century Renaissance-style building, designed by Sir Thomas Deane. It was originally built to house the collection of the Royal Dublin Society, the institution concerned with the implementation of Dublin's national museums and galleries. The National Library contains the world's largest collection of Irish documentary material: books, manuscripts, newspapers, periodicals, drawings, photographs and maps. Its mission is to collect and preserve these documents and to make them available to the public. It does not lend them out and all research has to take place in the reading rooms. The domed reading room on the first floor is particularly magnificent, and luminaries such as James Joyce worked here. You will need to get a reader's ticket to access any information, but it is free to look around. The library is most visited for its Genealogy Service (Mon–Fri 10–4:45, Sat 10–12:30) and family history research. There is a huge resource of Catholic parish records, 19th-century land valuations, trade and social directories, estate records and the largest collection of newspapers in Ireland, containing the all-important Births, Deaths and Marriages columns. The office of the Chief Herald and the Heraldic Museum (▶ 49) are also within the library. The huge collection of the National Photographic Archive has now moved to Temple Bar (▶ 71).

www.nli.ie
+ 29E2
✉ Kildare Street
☎ 603 0200
🕐 Mon–Wed 10–9, Thu–Fri 10–5, Sat 10–1
🚇 Pearse
🚌 Cross-city buses
♿ Good
💷 Free
↔ Heraldic Museum (▶ 49); National Gallery (▶ 22); National Museum (▶ 23)

Strolling past a striking curvilinear glasshouse in the National Botanic Gardens (left)

NATIONAL MUSEUM OF IRELAND (➤ 23, TOP TEN)

NATIONAL PRINT MUSEUM ★

An idiosyncratic little museum in a former soldiers' chapel houses a unique collection of objects related to the printing industry in Ireland. Much of the machinery is still in full working order. Guided tours make this a much more fun experience than it sounds. The processes of printing, from Gutenburg's Bible of 1455 through to the political printed material of the Easter Rising of 1916, are documented and the various methods of production and bookbinding explained. The guides, some of them retired printers, are very knowledgeable and dedicated to the art. Upstairs the walls are adorned with newspapers, showing the different styles of printed presentation and recalling major historic events in Ireland.

NATIONAL WAX MUSEUM ★

At Dublin's Wax Museum you can have fun as you gain a little more insight into the historical characters that have helped to shape Ireland's history. In the Hall of Megastars you will find popular entertainers, from Madonna and Elvis to Michael Jackson, and latest additions from the Irish music scene include U2. Younger children will enjoy the fairy-tales and legends brought to life, and you can learn more about Leonardo da Vinci through the impressive life-size replica of his painting, the *Last Supper*.

➕ Off map at 29F2
✉ Garrison Chapel, Beggar's Bush, Haddington Road
☎ 660 3770
🕐 Mon–Fri 10–5. Closed bank hols. Some weekend opening, check for details
🍴 Coffee shop (€)
🚇 Grand Canal Dock
🚌 7, 7A, 45
♿ Ground floor only
💰 Moderate

➕ 28C5
✉ Granby Row, Parnell Square
☎ 872 6340
🕐 Mon–Sat 10–5:30, Sun noon–5:30
🍴 Seated area with drinks machine (€)
🚌 Cross-city buses
♿ Few 💰 Expensive

The lavish Saloon in Newman House, St Stephen's Green (left)

NATURAL HISTORY MUSEUM ✪✪✪

For an original Victorian experience look no further than Dublin's fascinating Natural History Museum. It may be known as the city's 'Dead Zoo', but it gives a unique insight into the way Victorians treated the study and display of animals, and the values that went with that. You won't find interactives or touch-screen technology here; instead you will find antique displays showing some 10,000 stuffed animals – drawn from a collection of around 2,000,000 specimens. Some of them are in poor shape, while others are being replaced. The ground floor is devoted to Irish animals, including skeletons of the huge, extinct Irish deer or elk, complete with impressive antlers. The upper two floors display animals, birds, fish, reptiles, insects and invertebrates from around the world. A huge 20m (65ft) long skeleton of a humpback whale is suspended from the ceiling and there is the skeleton of the fascinating but sadly extinct dodo.

www.museum.ie
✚ 29E2
✉ Merrion Street
☎ 677 74444
🕐 Tue–Sat 10–5, Sun 2–5
🚆 Pearse
🚌 Cross-city buses
♿ Ground floor access only
💷 Free
↔ National Gallery (► 22), Number Twenty Nine (► 63)

Exhibition gallery inside the Natural History Museum (opposite)

NEWMAN HOUSE ✪✪

This is in fact two houses, both of them among the finest Georgian houses in Dublin. Cardinal Newman used the mansion in the 1850s to launch his great experiment to bring education to the Catholic masses. The Catholic University of Ireland was established here in 1865 and provided further education for men such as James Joyce and Eamon de Valera, who did not wish to attend the Protestant Trinity College. Newman House remains part of the original University, now known as University College Dublin. The houses are of particular interest for their spectacular plasterwork and superlative 18th-century interiors. Number 85 has work by Switzerland's great Lafranchini brothers, who decorated the walls and ceilings.

✚ 29D1
✉ 85–86 St Stephen's Green
☎ 716 7422
🕐 Jun–Aug, Tue–Fri, tours at noon, 2, 3, and 4
🚆 Pearse
🚌 Cross-city buses
♿ None
💷 Moderate
❓ Guided tours only
↔ University Church (► 72)

A Walk through Viking and Medieval Dublin

Distance
3km (2 miles)

Time
2 hours

Start point
Dublin Castle, Dame Street
➕ 28C3

End point
City Hall, Dame Street
➕ 28C3

Lunch
Queen of Tarts (➤ 96)

*St Patrick's Cathedral
is the largest church
in Ireland*

*From Dublin Castle (➤ 17) go up the hill and
turn left into Castle Street. At the end, go left
into Werburgh Street; St Werburgh's Church is
on the left.*

The 18th-century church, named after the King of Mercia's
daughter, was built on late 12th-century foundations.

*Continue down until you see St Patrick's
Cathedral (➤ 26) on your right. Cross the road
and pass the cathedral on your right. Turn right
into Kevin Street Upper; on the right is the
Garda Station, site of the Episcopal
Palace of St Sepulchre. Bear right
into St Patrick's Close, with its
medieval horse trough.*

There are great views on all sides of
St Patrick's Cathedral.

*Turn right up Patrick Street and
head towards Christ Church
Cathedral (➤ 16). Walk right
around the perimeter of the cathedral and follow
the cobbled lane at the back across into Cross
Lane South; on the left is Dvblinia (➤ 44).
Turn right into St Michael's Close and left into
Cook Street. On your left is St Audoen's arch
(1240), leading to St Audoen's churches
(➤ 66). Continue and go right into Bridge
Street Lower.*

On the left is the Brazen Head (➤ 92), the oldest pub in
Dublin.

*At the bridge, the site of the first Viking crossing,
turn right into Merchant's Quay and then
second right into Fishamble Street.*

Copper Alley, up the hill on the left (running through the
Harding Hotel), was one of the earliest Viking streets.

*Continue to the top and turn left into Lord
Edward Street, which filters into Dame Street;
opposite City Hall is the Queen of Tarts.*

NUMBER TWENTY NINE ★

Beautifully restored Number Twenty Nine is one of Dublin's Georgian jewels. It is laid out as the home of a middle-class family between 1790 and 1820, and offers a rare insight into the life of the period. An audio-visual show at the start of the tour introduces you to the family members, then leads from the servants' quarters in the basement to the attic playroom. Throughout are original artefacts and furnishings of the period, all recapturing the spirit of the age. It is the everyday items, in addition to some wonderful paintings, furnishings and plasterwork, that really bring this home to life.

- 🞥 29E2
- ✉ 29 Fitzwilliam Street Lower
- ☎ 702 6165
- ⏱ Tue–Sat 10–5, Sun 2–5
- 🍴 Tea room
- 🚉 Pearse
- 🚌 7, 10A, 13A
- ♿ None
- 👆 Moderate
- ↔ National Gallery (➤ 22), Natural History Museum (➤ 61)

O'CONNELL STREET ★★

O'Connell Street became Dublin's main thoroughfare in 1794 when O'Connell Bridge was built. Formerly known as Carlisle Bridge, it is one of the busiest crossings over the River Liffey. Highlights on the street include the General Post Office (➤ 18) and Dublin's famous department store, Clery's (➤ 104). A statue of Daniel O'Connell ('The Liberator' ➤ 14) is next to the bridge. You can still see bullet marks from the fighting in 1916. O'Connell Street is currently undergoing a much needed face-lift and one of its newest attractions is The Spire (also known as the Monument of Light, ➤ 70), erected in 2002.

- 🞥 29D4
- ✉ O'Connell Street
- 🚉 Tara Street
- 🚌 Cross-city buses

OLD JAMESON DISTILLERY ★★

This former distillery is in Smithfield Village (➤ 69), at the centre of the development of a once run-down area. The guided tour traces the history of Irish whiskey with exhibits and an audio-visual presentation. Whiskey was produced here from 1780 until 1971; it is now made in Middleton, County Cork. Learn everything there is to know about Irish whiskey and how it differs to Scotch whisky, and don't miss the free dram in the Jameson Bar at the end of the tour. There is a huge choice of whiskey products for sale in the distillery shop.

- www.whiskeytours.ie
- 🞥 28B4
- ✉ Bow Street, Smithfield
- ☎ 807 2355
- ⏱ Daily 9:30–6 (last tour at 5:30)
- 🍴 Restaurant, bar (€–€€)
- 🚉 Smithfield LUAS
- 🚌 68, 69, 79, 83, 90
- ♿ Good
- 👆 Expensive
- ❓ Gift shop

Discover the history of Irish whiskey at the Old Jameson Distillery

Oscar Wilde once lived in this elegant Georgian house on Merrion Square

www.amcd.edu
- 📍 29E2
- ✉ 1 Merrion Square
- ☎ 662 0281
- 🕐 Mon, Wed, Thu tours at 10:15 and 11:15
- 🚇 Pearse
- 🚌 Cross-city buses
- ♿ None
- 💷 Inexpensive
- ↔ National Gallery (➤ 22), National Library (➤ 59)

- 📍 28C4
- ✉ Parnell Square
- 🚇 Tara Street/Connolly
- 🚌 Cross-city buses

OSCAR WILDE'S HOUSE ✪

The home of writer Oscar Wilde from 1855 to 1876 is an excellent example of Georgian architecture. The restored house, on the north side of Merrion Square (➤ 58), with its remarkable cornices and architraves, was the first to be built on the square in 1762. In 1994 the American College Dublin took over the house and opened it for guided tours. Renovation involved the revival of traditional crafts to repair the plasterwork and restore the original stone and wooden floors. Use of period paints, antique furnishings and reproduction Georgian furniture have given a first-class result.

PARNELL SQUARE ✪

Laid out in 1755, this is the city's oldest Georgian square after St Stephen's Green (➤ 68). Today it is a shadow of its former glory, but it still holds many points of interest, including the Gate Theatre (➤ 47) and the Garden of Remembrance (open during daylight). This peaceful garden is dedicated to those who gave their lives for Irish independence. The focal point is the large bronze *Children of Lír* sculpture by Oisín Kelly. Other highlights in the square are the Dublin Writers Museum (➤ 42–43), the Hugh Lane Art Gallery (➤ 52) and the 1758 Rotunda Hospital, the oldest maternity hospital in the world.

PHOENIX PARK ⭐⭐

Phoenix Park is one of the largest city parks in Europe, if not the world, covering some 696ha (1,720 acres), and is encircled by a 13km (8-mile) wall. It was created in 1663, following instructions from King Charles II to provide a deer park. In 1745 it opened to the public and has been popular with Dubliners and visitors ever since. Ireland's tallest monument (63m/206ft), commemorating the Duke of Wellington's victory at Waterloo in 1815, can be found here, not far from the excellent Dublin Zoo (➤ 43). There's a lively historical interpretation of the park at the visitor centre and a children's exhibition on forest wildlife.

Adjoining the centre is Ashtown Castle, a medieval tower house complete with miniature maze. On the northern side of the park stands Áras an Uachtaráin, the official residence of the President of Ireland, built in the Palladian style in 1751 (guided tours every Saturday). The rest of the park, with its woodland, lakes and gardens, is a great place to stroll and watch the world go by. Sports include Gaelic football, as well as running and cycling trails. Horse-riding, hurling and polo are for members only.

ROYAL COLLEGE OF SURGEONS ⭐

This internationally renowned institution is in one of the city's best Georgian buildings, overlooking St Stephen's Green (➤ 68). Designed by architect Edward Parke, it dates from 1806 and has a neo-classical granite façade and distinctive round-headed windows. The three statues above the pediment are of Hygieia (goddess of health), Asclepius (god of medicine) and Athena (goddess of wisdom). The building was commandeered by Irish Volunteers under the leadership of Countess Markievicz in the 1916 Easter Rising, and you can still see the bullet marks on the façade.

🔳 Off map at 28A3
🚉 Heuston LUAS
🚌 10A, 25, 25A, 26, 66, 66A, 66B

Phoenix Park Visitor Centre
✉ Phoenix Park
☎ 677 0095
🕐 Park open daylight hours. Visitor centre: Apr–Sep, daily 10–6; mid- to end Mar, 10–5:30; Oct, 10–5; Nov to mid-Mar, Sat–Sun 10–5
🍴 Restaurant and Café (€€–€)
♿ Park good; visitor centre only ground floor accessible
💷 Park free; visitor centre moderate
❓ Free tickets for tours of Áras an Uachtaráin available at visitor centre

---

🔳 29D2
✉ 123 St Stephen's Green
☎ 402 2248
🕐 By appointment only
🚉 Pearse Street
🚌 Cross-city buses
♿ Few
💷 Free
❓ Guided tours on request

The Pheonix Column in Phoenix Park

29D2
✉ Dawson Street
☎ 676 7727
⏱ Mon–Fri 10–4 and
  Sunday service
🚉 Pearse Street
🚌 Cross-city buses
♿ Good
🎫 Free

*The exquisite nave of St
Ann's Church*

ST ANN'S CHURCH ⊕

For the best view of this striking church, founded in 1707, look down Anne Street South from Grafton Street. The church was created for the rapidly evolving Georgian suburbs occupied by wealthy and influential residents. Its stunning Romanesque façade was added in 1868 by architects Deane and Woodward. Inside is a series of colourful stained-glass windows dating from the mid-19th century. It was here that the 18th-century nationalist leader Wolf Tone was married in 1785, as was Bram Stoker, the author of *Dracula*, in 1878. St Ann's has a long tradition of charity work; in 1723 Baron Butler left a bequest to provide 120 loaves of bread each week for the poor, and today anyone may take a loaf from the shelf beside the altar.

 77F3
✉ Clontarf/Raheny
⏱ Summer, daily 9–7;
  winter, 10–dusk
🚉 Killester
🚌 130
♿ Good
🎫 Free

ST ANNE'S PARK ⊕

St Anne's Park, in the northern suburbs of Dublin, was once the home of the Guinness family. The grounds were acquired by Dublin Corporation in 1939, and the house, which was gutted by fire, was finally demolished in 1968. The park covers some 112ha (276 acres) and consists of extensive woodlands, hidden walled gardens, follies, a mile-long avenue of stately oaks that originally led up to the house, and the famous rose garden. This glorious park opened to the public in 1975 and is best viewed between June and September. There are also many sporting facilities, including football pitches, tennis courts and a 12-hole golf course.

✚ 28B3
✉ Cornmarket, High Street
☎ 677 0088
⏱ Daily 9:30–5:30 (no
  admission after 4:45)
🚌 Cross-city buses
♿ Church good; visitor
  centre only ground floor
  accessible
🎫 Inexpensive

ST AUDOEN'S CHURCHES ⊕

The two churches dedicated to St Audoen – originally known as St Ouen – bishop of Rouen and patron saint of Normandy, stand side by side in the heart of the old medieval city. The most interesting is the Protestant St Audoen, the only surviving medieval parish church in Dublin. It is believed there has been a church here since the 9th century, but the tower and door of this version dates from the 12th century. The nave was added in the 15th century and three of the bells date from 1423. Look for the restored memorials to the Sparke and Duff families. An exhibition explaining the importance of St Audoen's in the life of medieval Dublin is on display in the Guild Chapel of St Anne. The adjoining Roman Catholic Church of St Audoen was built between 1841 and 1847.

ST MICHAN'S CHURCH

Not for the faint-hearted, this church hides a gory secret in its crypt. The dry atmosphere caused bodies to mummify rather than decompose and, although the old coffins deteriorated and split open over time, the bodies remained intact, complete with hair and skin. A guided tour will show you this gruesome sight, with stories of those buried here, including the leaders of the 1798 rebellion, and barristers John and Henry Sheares. You can also see Wolfe Tone's death mask. The origins of the church can be traced back to 1095, although the current building was constructed in 1686. Inside highlights include an organ believed to have been played by Handel and attractive woodcarvings of fruits and musical instruments above the choir.

ST PATRICK'S CATHEDRAL (► 26, TOP TEN)

✚ 28B3
✉ Church Street
☎ 872 4154
🕐 Mar–Oct, Mon–Fri 10–12:30, 2–4:30, Sat 10–12.45; Nov–Feb, Mon–Fri 12:30–2:30
🚇 Smithfield LUAS
🚌 83
♿ Few
👆 Moderate
❓ Access to vaults by tour only

Open caskets reveal the mummified remains of those laid to rest in the crypt of St Michan's Church, Dublin

ST STEPHEN'S GREEN

✚ 29D2

✉ St Stephen's Green, at top of Grafton Street

🕐 Mon–Sat 8–dusk, Sun & public hols 10–dusk

🚃 Pearse

🚌 Cross-city buses

♿ Very good

💲 Free

St Stephen's Green (above) is popular with both locals and visitors

The James Joyce Tower, Sandycove (below)

This pleasant park is one of the most famous in central Dublin. Once common ground where public hangings, whippings and burnings took place, today the 9ha (22-acre) green is a popular lunchtime venue for office and shop workers and a haven for visitors when sightseeing gets a bit too much. The duck pond, attractive flower beds and beautiful garden for the blind create a sanctuary from the city. The green was landscaped in the 18th century and St Stephen's became much sought after by the wealthy, who began to build their glorious Georgian town houses around the central park. Trees and paths, railings and gates were installed and you could have access to the green at an annual cost of one guinea. The public were allowed free access again following an act of parliament proposed by Sir Arthur Guinness in 1877. The north side, known as Beaux Walk in the 18th-century, is still the most fashionable part, overlooked by the exclusive Shelbourne Hotel (► 101). Highlights are the Fusliers' Arch at the Grafton Street entrance, the Three Fates Fountain and the modern memorial, near Merrion Row, to the nationalist Wolfe Tone, better known locally as Tonehenge. Notable buildings around the green include the Royal College of Surgeons (► 65) and Newman House (► 61).

SANDYCOVE AND JAMES JOYCE TOWER ⓞⓞ

James Joyce Museum

✚ 77F3

✉ James Joyce Tower, Sandycove

☎ 280 9265

🕐 Apr–Oct, Mon–Sat 10–1, 2–5, Sun & public hols 2–6

🚃 Sandycove

🚌 59 from Dun Laoghaire

♿ None

💲 Moderate

Just south of Dun Laoghaire (pronounced Dun Leary) is the affluent village and popular commuter suburb of Sandycove. It is named after a small sandy cove near the rocky point on which a Martello tower was built in 1804 to withstand a threatened invasion by Napoleon along this coastline. James Joyce stayed in the tower for a week and it features in the opening chapter of his famous novel *Ulysses*. It now houses a small museum of Joycean memorabilia, Including a collection of letters, photographs, first and rare editions and personal possessions of the author, including his guitar and walking stick. If you fancy a swim, directly below the tower is the Forty Foot Pool (complete with changing areas), traditionally an all-male nude bathing pool, but now open to both sexes; swimming costumes permitted!

Playwright George Bernard Shaw was born in this house (left) in 1856

Enjoy views over Dublin from the top of the Chimney at Smithfield (below)

SHAW'S BIRTHPLACE ⭐

'Author of many plays' is the simple accolade on the plaque outside the birthplace of George Bernard Shaw, the famous playwright. This restored Victorian home, close to the Grand Canal, reflects the life of a 19th-century middle-class family and was a source of inspiration for many of the characters Shaw would use later in his plays. You can see the drawing room where Shaw's mother held her musical soirees, the front parlour and the children's bedrooms. Shaw was born here in 1856, leaving 20 years later to live in London.

➕ 28C1
✉ 33 Synge Street
☎ 475 0854
🕐 May–Sep, Mon–Tue & Thu–Fri 10–1, 2–5, Sat–Sun & public hols 2–5
🚌 16, 16A, 19, 19A, 122
♿ Few
💷 Expensive
↔ Grand Canal (► 48)

SMITHFIELD ⭐⭐

It's still all happening at Smithfield, the once run-down corner of the city. Redevelopment and rejuvenation of the old cattle market began in the early 1990s and there is still lots going on. Central to the 'village' is the Old Jameson Distillery (► 63), no longer in production but running successful tours and selling whiskey-related merchandise. Towering over the whole area is the 56m (184ft) high Chimney (► 110), built by the Jameson company in 1895. You can take a ride to the top for panoramic views over Dublin. Duck Lane, with its restaurant and interior design shops, opens onto a new cobbled plaza featuring floodlights and overhead gas heaters. New apartments are being built, with the promise of more restaurants and bars in the future.

➕ 28B4
✉ Smithfield Village
🚇 Smithfield LUAS
🚌 83
💷 Expensive

DID YOU KNOW?

James Joyce's brief stay in the Martello tower at Sandycove was the inspiration for his blockbusting novel *Ulysses* (the first chapter is set in the tower). The main living room inside and the gun platform with its fine views are much as he described them in his book.

69

➕ 29D4
✉ O'Connell Street
🚇 Tara Street
🚌 Cross-city buses
↔ General Post Office
(►18)

THE SPIRE ✪✪

The Spire, also known as the Monument of Light, was unveiled in O'Connell Street in 2002. It has been erected across the road from the General Post Office on the site where Nelson's Column used to be. Made of light reflective stainless steel, the Spire is 120m (394ft) high, 3m (10ft) in diameter at the base and only 15cm (6 inches) at the top. It rises majestically above the rooftops where it sways gently (but safely) in the breeze. It is central to the rejuvenation of this somewhat down-at-heel area.

➕ 28C3
✉ Essex Quay
🕐 View from outside only
🚌 Cross-city buses

SUNLIGHT CHAMBERS ✪

On the corner of Essex Quay and Parliament Street, on the south side of the river, stands Sunlight Chambers. It was built at the turn of the 20th century as the Dublin offices of Lever Brothers by Liverpool architect Edward Ould, who also designed Port Sunlight. The building has unusual Italianate terracotta friezes that advertise the company's product – soap. In fact, they depict the history of hygiene. In its early years the building was unpopular because a 'foreign' architect had been employed, and upon its completion a journal called *The Irish Builder* referred to it as the 'ugliest building in Dublin'.

An internet café (below)

Shopping at the Saturday food market in Meeting House Square (right)

TEMPLE BAR ●●●

The area known as Temple Bar is sandwiched between Dame Street and the River Liffey and covers some 11ha (27 acres). Its origins can be traced back to Anglo-Irish Sir William Temple, who bought the land bounding the river in the 16th century and who liked to promenade with his family by the river. The word 'bar' means riverside path. The area gradually fell into decline as the low depth of the Liffey forced the docks area eastwards and Temple Bar sank into decay, its dark alleys harbouring the poorest citizens of Ireland. In the late 1970s, the land was acquired by Ireland's state transport company CIE, who had plans to build a huge bus depot on the site. While plans were being discussed the company rented out some of the derelict properties to artists, musicians and artisans.

In the 1980s, the residents and artists formed a lobbying group and set about trying to save Temple Bar, fighting for the preservation of the buildings in the area. The Irish government supported the cause and an organisation called Temple Bar Properties was created to co-ordinate and administer the project; their new information centre opened in early 2004. The progress made in ten years is staggering. This is now the cultural centre of the city and the place to go for shopping, socialising, eating and drinking. The public open-air spaces, such as Meeting House Square, showcase Irish artistic talent, be it art, music or juggling. Streets a little further afield have also been brought under the Temple Bar umbrella, such as Cow's Lane, with its design shops, which has been redeveloped and pedestrianised. Temple Bar was almost too successful for its own good – with the stag and hen party revellers overspilling from the bars and restaurants, the residents and corporation believed the area was losing its way and gaining a reputation for over indulgence and drunken debauchery. It still gets a bit rowdy at the weekends for some, but during the day and weekday nights it's a great place to be. Among the principal arts venues are the Temple Bar Music Centre (➤ 113), the National Photographic Archive, Gallery of Photography, Temple Bar Gallery and Studios and the Ark Children's Cultural Centre (➤ 110).

✚ 29D3
🚉 Tara Street
🚌 Cross-city buses

Temple Bar Information Centre
www.templebar.ie
✉ 12 East Essex Street, Temple Bar
🕐 Mon–Fri 9–5:30 (also Jun–Sep, Sat 10–6, Sun 12:30–4:30)

Chilling out in Temple Bar (above)

TRINITY COLLEGE (► 24–25, TOP TEN)

UNIVERSITY CHURCH ✪✪

🕂 29D1
✉ 87A St Stephen's Green
☎ 478 1606
🕙 Mon–Sat 9–5:30, Sun 10–1, 5–6
🚆 Pearse
🚌 Cross-city buses
♿ None
🖐 Free
↔ Newman House (► 61)

It's easy to miss the front entrance to this church, which is next door to Newman House in St Stephen's Green. If you can find it, beyond the small entrance porch is a remarkable Byzantine-style interior. Commissioned by Cardinal Newman in 1856 – who disliked the Gothic style of the time – the church was built on the garden plot between No 86 and No 87. The nave is richly decorated

with Irish marble slabs and there is an ornate canopy over the altar. Look out for the little birds on the capitals of the columns dividing the marble panels. John Hungerford Pollen, architect and friend of Newman, came over from England to supervise the building and also painted the elaborate ceiling. The lighting is subdued, the church lit by small windows set under the roof, and the whole atmosphere is one of calm and tranquillity. University Church is a popular venue for student marriages.

The unusual entrance to University Church

WAR MEMORIAL GARDENS ✪✪

🕂 Off map at 28A3
✉ Islandbridge
☎ 677 0236
🕙 Mon–Fri 8–dusk, Sat–Sun 10–dusk
🚆 Pearse
🚌 25, 25A, 51, 66, 66A, 66B, 69
♿ Good
🖐 Free
↔ Kilmainham Gaol (► 21), Phoenix Park (► 65)

These gardens are well off the tourist track, on the southern bank of the River Liffey opposite Phoenix Park. They are dedicated to the memory of the 49,400 Irish soldiers who died in World War I. The names of all the soldiers are contained in the two granite book rooms at either end of the gardens. Designed by the celebrated architect Sir Edwin Lutyens, this moving place is well worth a visit. With herbaceous borders, sunken rose gardens and extensive tree planting, the gardens are enjoyable at any time of year.

DID YOU KNOW?

St Valentine, patron saint of lovers, is buried in Whitefriars. His remains were brought from Rome in 1836 as a gift from Pope Gregory XVI in recognition of the preaching of the Irish Carmelite John Spratt. The bones are in a casket underneath a marble altar. Couples come here to pray and there are special blessing services held on his feast day, 14 February.

WATERWAYS ISLAND VISITOR CENTRE ✪

This centre, at Grand Canal Quay, is known to locals as 'the box in the docks' because of its distinct shape. The centre recounts the 200 years of the Grand's transition from its original use as a commercial waterway to its present-day recreational role using working models, audio-visual displays and information panels. It also includes examples of art and literature inspired by the waterways. A new marina is being built close to the centre, part of an on-going project for the canal dock area.

🚺 29F2
✉ Waterways Island Visitor Centre: Grand Canal Quay
☎ 677 7510
🕐 Jun–Sep, daily 9:30–5:30; Oct–May, Wed–Sun 12:30–5
🚊 Grand Canal Dock
🚌 2, 3
♿ Good; ground floor only
💷 Inexpensive

Our Lady of Dublin sacred shrine at the Whitefriars Carmelite Church

WHITEFRIARS CARMELITE CHURCH & ST VALENTINE'S SHRINE ✪

This church is run by the Carmelite order, who returned from abroad in 1827 to re-establish a church in the city. There had been a priory on the site when it was seized during the Reformation in the 16th century. One of the best-loved churches in Dublin, it contains the relics of St Valentine, the patron saint of lovers. Valentine died in Rome, but his remains were finally returned to his native Ireland in 1836 and are kept in a shrine to the right of the high altar. Note the unusual oak statue of the Virgin (Our Lady of Dublin), the only surviving wooden statue from the sacking of Ireland's monasteries during the Reformation.

🚺 28C2
✉ 56 Aungier Street
☎ 475 8821
🍴 Coffee shop (€)
🕐 Mon, Wed–Fri 7:45am–6pm, Tue 7:45am–9:15pm, Sat–Sun 7:45am–7:30pm. Closed pm on public hols
🚊 Pearse
🚌 Cross-city buses
♿ Good
💷 Free

73

Around Dublin

From fine country houses and gardens to prehistoric tombs, from mountains, lakes and valleys to splendid golf courses – there is something for everyone in the eastern counties around Dublin. The pace of life is slower than in the city and you will need a car to visit the more remote areas, but many of the main attractions can be reached by public transport. To the southwest are the rolling green fields of County Kildare, an area famous for horse breeding and its racecourse, the Curragh. South are the wild peaks of the Wicklow Mountains, where there are great opportunities for walking and touring. To the north the extraordinary ancient burial sites at Brú Na Bóinne dominate County Meath and further north in County Louth is the site of the famous Battle of the Boyne of 1690.

> ' *Sweet vale of Avoca! How calm could I rest, in thy bosom of shade with the ones I love best.* '

THOMAS MOORE
The Meeting of the Waters (1807)

———————— ● ————————

The entrance stone to the passage grave at Newgrange (left)

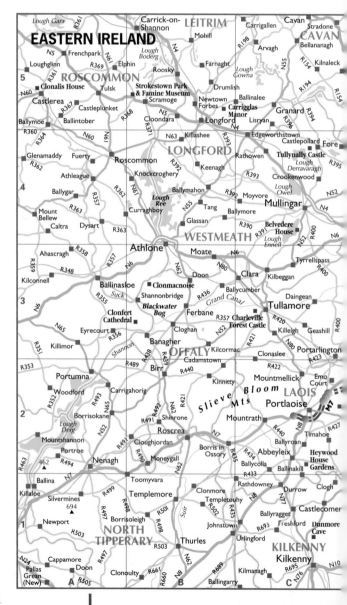

www.avoca.ie

✚ 77F1

✉ Old Mill, Avoca, Co Wicklow

☎ 0402 35105

🕐 Daily 9–6 (9:30–5:30 in winter)

🚌 Bus Éireann 133 to Avoca (bus sevice is infrequent)

♿ Good

🖐 Free

AVOCA HANDWEAVERS ★★

This is a remarkable rural Irish business success dating back to the early 1700s. Located in the heart of County Wicklow, in the village of Avoca, the handweavers began spinning and weaving blankets and clothing in 1723. With the invention of the fly shuttle loom – a style of loom still used today – the weavers were able to produce up to 20m (22 yards) of cloth per day. The business, however, did not really flourish until the 1920s, when the Wynne sisters inherited the mill and with flair and ingenuity built an excellent business marketing tweeds all over the world, supplying top-class designers and even selling to royalty. The business expanded with the introduction of rugs and throws using natural fibres, including lambswool and cashmere in a brilliant range of colours. You can visit the mill to see production in progress and hopefully pick up a bargain in the factory shop. Avoca Handweavers has been managed by the Pratt family since 1974 and has expanded into homeware, cookbooks, cafés, a chic designer range of clothes called Anthology and a garden centre and nursery. Its department store in Suffolk Street, in Dublin, has a wide selection of products on offer (▶ 104). The village of Avoca has another claim to fame – it was the location for the popular BBC television drama *Ballykissangel*.

The cloisters at Bective Abbey (above)

✚ 77E4

✉ Bective, Navan, Co Meath

☎ 046 943 7227

🕐 Daily, daylight hours

🚌 Bus Éireann service 109 Dublin to Navan, then 135 Navan to Scurloughstown stops at Bective Cross

♿ Poor

🖐 Free

BECTIVE ABBEY ★

The original abbey was built in 1147 by Murchad, King of Meath, as the sister house to the main Cistercian Abbey at Mellifont in County Leath. Little of the early building survives today and what you can see in a field by the River Boyne is really the ruin of a 15th-century fortified building – more castle than monastery. The abbey was repressed in 1536 and after a series of lay owners fell into disrepair. What remains gives an indication of a religious, defensive and domestic building. The religious aspects are the cloisters – the best-preserved part of the building – the nave and the chapter house. The defensive parts can be seen in the square tower and the domestic parts in the remains of fireplaces, chimneys and windows. There are plenty of passageways, staircases and chambers to explore and good spots for a picnic.

Colourful boats moored in Bray harbour (opposite)

BRAY ⊛⊛

From a one-street town in the 1830s, Bray is now home to over 27,000 people, many of whom commute daily by DART into Dublin. This former refined Victorian seaside resort has become a playground for families and day-trippers. The safe, sand and shingle beach stretches for 1.5km (1 mile) and can get very crowded in summer. You might prefer to walk along the cliffs at Bray Head, which at 241m (790ft) above the sea offer great views. On the seafront is the fascinating conservation-conscious National Sealife Centre (▶ 111). Other activities in Bray include golf, sailing and fishing. Alternatively you can just wander along the esplanade that stretches from Bray Harbour to Bray Head and watch the world go by.

Just outside the town, at the foot of the Little Sugar Loaf mountain, is beautiful **Kilruddery House and Gardens**, home to the Brabazon family since 1618. The house was originally built in the 17th century, but was remodelled in Elizabethan style in the 1820s. There are carvings by Grinling Gibbons and furniture by Chippendale, and a lovely Orangery, added in 1852, has some remarkable marble statues. The superb gardens, the oldest formal gardens in Ireland, were created in the 1680s in the French style. Kilruddery hosts open-air theatre and classical music concerts.

✚ 77F3
🚉 Bray
🚌 45, 84

Tourist Information
✉ Old Courthouse, Main Street Bray, Co Wicklow
☎ 286 7128

Kilruddery House and Gardens
www.kilruddery.com
✉ Bray
☎ 286 3405
🕐 Gardens: Apr–Sep, daily 1–5; house: May, Jun, Sep, daily 1–5
🚉 Bray, then Finnegan bus stops close to entrance
🚌 84 from Dublin stops at Woodlands Hotel, then short walk to entrance
♿ Few
👋 House and garden: expensive; garden only: moderate

BRÚ NA BÓINNE

The Boyne Valley is strewn with some of Ireland's most important archaeological monuments. Brú Na Bóinne (Palace of the Boyne), a designated UNESCO World Heritage Site, has Europe's richest concentration of ancient monuments, including forts, henges, standing stones and the mysterious grand passage tombs of Newgrange, Knowth and Dowth. To understand the significance of the site you need to realise that these monuments are 1,000 years older than England's Stonehenge and 100 years older than the pyramids of Giza in Egypt. The River Boyne valley was first settled during the Stone Age and it is possible the pre-Celtic founders may have come from the Iberian Peninsula, but many other legends surround the site. Take a look around the visitor centre for background information before embarking on a tour. In high summer you should book well in advance as the tours are restricted to 700 visitors a day.

Newgrange

Newgrange was probably built more than 5,000 years ago by extremely skilled builders. This is evident from the excellent condition of the tombs. The spectacular passage grave here is the high point of a visit. Built into a giant mound 85m (280ft) across and 10m (33ft) high, its perimeter is defined by nearly a hundred massive kerbstones. The exterior is faced with brilliant white quartzite. At least 200,000 tons of stone went into its construction, with stones as large as 16 tons each brought from as far away as County Wicklow. At the entrance to the tomb one of these kerbstones is marked with the distinctive spiral details of this area and above it is a rectangular opening like a mail box. It is through this roof box that the dawn light enters at the winter solstice and shines through to the interior. A lottery system gives people the chance to witness this event, otherwise you will have to make do with with a simulated experience. A guide leads you

The Knowth burial mound (above)

by torchlight along the 19m (62-foot) long passage into the heart of the mound and to the burial chamber with its intricate corbelled ceiling rising 6m (20 feet) above you. Here is the most amazing spiral abstract carved detail in the walls. When the tomb was excavated only a few bodies were found, unusual considering the tomb's size. It is possible that remains were removed regularly.

Knowth

You can see the great tomb of Knowth from the road, but you can access it only by taking a tour. This mound is defined by some 120 kerbstones and is surrounded by at least 17 small passage graves. Inside the main tomb (closed to visitors) are two passages and the stonework is rich with spiral and line carvings. What could be the significance of these zigzags and whorls? The exterior is also beautifully decorated.

Dowth

Dowth is a significant site and contains some of the finest rock carvings to be seen anywhere in Ireland. It can be viewed from the road to the east of Newgrange. The passage grave here was heavily excavated by the Victorians and became popular with souvenir hunters.

- 77E4
- Donore, Co Meath
- 041 988 0300/0305
- Mar–Apr, daily 9:30–5:30; May, 9–6:30; Jun to mid-Sep, 9–7; mid-Sep to end Sep, 9–6:30; Oct, 9:30–5; Nov–Feb, 9:30–5. Knowth open: May–Oct only
- Tea room at visitor centre (€)
- Bus Éireann 100 Dublin to Drogheda, then 163 to Donore village (10 min walk)
- Visitor centre good; monuments poor
- Varies according to site; visitor centre only: inexpensive
- Access to monuments by tour only, lasting 1 hour 15 min (allow at least 3 hours if visiting both Newgrange and Knowth). The last tour departs 1 hour 45 min before the centre closes but it is best to visit early as it is often oversubscribed and visitors are regularly turned away.

Dazzling white quartzite enhances the burial mound at Newgrange (left)

🚩 77E3

✉ Celbridge, Co Kildare

☎ 628 8252

🕐 Easter Sun–Sep, Mon–Fri 10–6, Sat, Sun and public hols 1–6; Oct, Mon–Fri 10–5, Sun and public hols 1–5

🍴 Coffee shop (€)

🚌 67, 67A, 67N, 67X

♿ Lower floors good, otherwise poor

💰 Moderate

❓ Guided tour only, lasts approximately 1 hour

CASTLETOWN HOUSE ⭐

This striking house was built in the Palladian style between 1722 and 1732 for the Speaker of the Irish Parliament and at the time Ireland's richest man, William Connolly. Starting life in humble circumstances, Connolly amassed his wealth by buying and selling forfeited property in the aftermath of the Battle of the Boyne in 1690. Castletown's opulent interior has elaborate rococo stucco work by the Francini brothers and a Long Gallery decorated in the Pompeian style of the 1770s. Look out for the huge painting called *The Boar Hunt* by Paul de Vos (1569–1679) in the main hall. Connolly did not see the project through and died before the house was completed; his widow continued improvements. Her main contribution was Connolly's Folly, an unusual obelisk structure some 40m (130ft) high, 3km (2 miles) north of the house. The magnificent interiors of the house were subsequently completed by Lady Louisa Connolly, wife of William Connolly's great nephew, who moved here in 1759. One fascinating room is the Print Room, lined with elaborately framed prints from 18th-century magazines.

🚩 77E4

🚌 Bus Éireann service 163 to Drogheda

🚂 Drogheda

Tourist Information

✉ Bus Éireann Depot, Donore Road, Drogheda, Co Louth

☎ 041 983 7070

Millmount Museum

✉ Millmount Square, Drogheda, Co Louth

☎ 041 983 3097

🕐 Mon–Sat 10–6, Sun & public hols 2:30–6

♿ Good

💰 Moderate

DROGHEDA ⭐

The town of Drogheda stands at the lowest bridging point of the River Boyne, just a few kilometres from the site of the famous Battle of the Boyne in 1690. It was first established by Viking traders in 911 and was an important Norman port in the 14th century. Little remains of the

A sailing boat on the River Boyne at Drogheda (right)

town walls but there are still elements of medieval architecture in the hilly streets, including St Lawrence's Gate, a fine four-storey barbican. Also of interest is the Magdalene Tower, the only remains of the original Dominican friary of 1224. Above the south bank of the river – accessed from the riverside by steep steps – is the Norman motte, topped by a Martello tower (c1808), with splendid views over the town. It is also the site of the **Millmount Museum**, housed in the old barracks, with exhibits relating to the town and its industries, an authentic 19th-century kitchen and a craft centre showcasing Irish design, including jewellery, knitwear and ceramics.

GLENDALOUGH   ✪✪✪

Deep in the heart of the Wicklow Mountains are the atmospheric remains of a remarkable monastic settlement founded in the 6th century by St Kevin, who came from one of Leinster's ruling families. He was abbot of Glendalough until his death in AD 618 and the monastery became famous throughout Europe as a seat of learning. It remained an important place of pilgrimage well into the 18th century. The site is one of Ireland's premier attractions and can get very busy in high summer; the best time to visit is a quiet spring or autumn evening. The setting is magnificent, with the lake and the mountains making a superb backdrop, and the area is particularly popular with walkers. The ruins incorporate a 12th-century round tower and the 11th-century St Kevin's Church, known as St

Kevin's Kitchen, possibly because the belfry tower resembles a chimney. The roofless cathedral of St Peter and St Paul dates from the 12th century and is the largest ruin. There are several other churches and monastic buildings around the site, as well as numerous gravestones and crosses. Some of the remains, although visible from the shore, are accessible only by boat, including the Tempull na Skellig or 'church on the rock' and St Kevin's Bed, a small cave reputed to have been the saint's retreat. The visitor centre, also the information centre for the Wicklow Mountains National Park (➤ 89), has an audio-visual presentation to the site, and its interactive displays give a good insight into the life and times of St Kevin and the monastery.

🔒 77E2
🚌 Glendalough bus twice daily from Bray and Dublin

Visitor Centre
✉ Glendalough, Bray, Co Wicklow
☎ 0404 45325/45352
🕐 Daily 9:30–5:15
♿ Visitor centre very good, otherwise poor
✋ Inexpensive
❓ Guided tour on request, lasts 30–40 min

The Magdalene Tower in Drogheda (above)

A Drive Through the Wicklow Mountains

Distance
150km (93 miles)

Time
Allow a day

Start/end point
Dublin
✚ 77E3

Lunch
Downshire House,
Blessington (➤ 99)

*Gravestones and crosses
at Glendalough, County
Wicklow (above)*

*Pick up the N11 out of Dublin and head south
on the M11 to Bray, turning right onto the
R117 for Enniskerry and Powerscourt House
and Gardens (➤ 87).*

The house is on a bend at the end of the village. The
gardens are among the finest in Europe and Powerscourt
Waterfall is Ireland's highest.

*Return to Enniskerry, and turn left; after 8km
(5 miles) you reach Glencree. At the next
junction head for Sally Gap, Glendalough. After
another 8km (5 miles) turn right, and keep
following signs for Blessington until you reach
the N81. Go left and after 3km (2 miles) turn
left on to the R758, signposted Valleymount,
Lake Drive. Continue, following signs for
Glendalough (➤ 83).*

St Kevin established a monastic settlement here at the
valley of the two loughs in the 6th century; it is one of
the most beautiful spots in Ireland.

*Return to the junction and continue through
Laragh. After 5km (3 miles) turn right,
signposted Arklow, Rathdrum (R755). In
Rathdrum follow signs for Avoca. At the T-
junction, turn left, then bear right, signposted to
Dublin. After 13km (8 miles) turn right for
Wicklow.*

Wicklow is the county town and the centre of the area
known as the Garden of Ireland.

*Leave Wicklow on the Dublin road and
continue to Ashford.*

Mount Usher Gardens, off to the right along the banks of
the River Vartry, are a superb example of 'wild gardens'.

*In Ashford turn left, then fork right, following
signs for Roundwood. At the T-junction by
Roundwood church, turn left, then right for
Enniskerry. Continue to the village. From here
take the return route to Dublin.*

HILL OF TARA ⭐

At first sight it may seem as if you are looking at a few grassy humps and depressions in the landscape, but it is worth the trip, not just for the superb views, but for the sense of history and mythology evoked by this important neolithic place. Tara was the main religious and political centre of Ireland during the first millennium AD, where priests and kings would gather. It remained the seat of the High Kings until the 6th century; although its connection to royalty remained until the 11th century, its importance was waning by this time with the spread of Christianity. Among the more impressive remains is the Mound of Hostages, a passage grave that, on excavation, revealed 40 Bronze Age cremations from around 2000BC. One of the most prominent earthworks is the Royal Enclosure with a ring fort known as Cormac's House in the centre. Here stands a pillar, known as Lia Faíl, or Stone of Destiny, where the High Kings of Ireland were crowned. There is a visitor centre on site in St Patrick's Church (open summer only), with an audio-visual display and tours of the site.

KELLS ⭐

You probably wouldn't visit the town of Kells if it wasn't for its connection with the famous book, and a visit to the heritage centre puts the Book of Kells and the monastery into historical context. A monastery was founded here as early as AD 550, but it was not until the early 9th century that the monks came with their famous illuminated manuscript from the island of Iona, having fled the Viking raids. The work was completed in Kells and the displays in the heritage centre allow you to view the pages on computer and see how the town appeared in those early days. The book is now on display at Dublin's Trinity College Library (➤ 24–25), but there are some good replicas here to view.

Sheep grazing on top of the ancient Hill of Tara (left)

☩ 77E4
✉ Near Navan, Co Meath
☎ 046 90 25903
⏰ Main site open during daylight hours. Visitor centre in St Patrick's Church mid-May to mid-Sep, daily 10–6
🍽 Café near site (€)
🚌 Bus Éireann service 109 to Tara Cross (ask driver for stop)
♿ Poor
💶 Inexpensive
❓ Guided tours, last 40 minutes

The intricate South Cross (left) stands in the middle of the town of Kells

---

☩ 77D5
🚌 Bus Éireann service 109 to Kells

Kells Heritage Centre

✉ The Courthouse, Headfort Place, Kells, Co Meath
☎ 046 92 47840
⏰ May–Sep, Mon–Sat 10–5:30, Sun & public hols 1:30–6; Oct–Apr, Tue–Sat 10–5
🍽 Café (€)
♿ Good
💶 Moderate

77D3

Bus Éireann service 126 to Kildare

Kildare

Tourist Information

Market House, Market Square, Co. Kildare

045 521240

Mon–Fri 10–1, 2–5

Irish National Stud/ Japanese Gardens/ St Fiachra's Garden

Tully, Kildare

045 521617

Mid-Feb to mid-Nov, daily 9:30–6

Restaurant (€€)

Bus Éireann service 126 to Kildare, stops at gate

Kildare

National Stud and St Fiachra's Garden good, Japanese Garden poor

Expensive (covers both gardens and National Stud)

Guided tour to National Stud, allow one hour

KILDARE ⭐⭐

Since this attractive town got its bypass in 2003, the centre has become pleasantly quiet. In the old Market House is the tourist information office, and a heritage centre that traces the history of Kildare and its surroundings. The town is dominated by St Brigid's Cathedral, built on the site of a former monastery founded in AD 490. The original 10th-century tower survives and is an impressive 33m (108ft) high.

County Kildare is horseracing country and the home of the famous racecourse, the Curragh. Just south of Kildare is Tully House and the **Irish National Stud**, which was founded in 1900 by Colonel William Hall-Walker; now a state-run stud, it breeds some of the most famous racehorses in the world. The best time to visit the stables is between February and July, when there can be as many as 300 foals on view. Tours of the stable blocks and paddocks are available and there is a Horse Museum illustrating the importance of horses and racing to the Irish nation. Look out for the skeleton of Arkle, one of the stud's most famous champion stallions.

The Japanese Gardens at Tully House, landscaped between 1906 and 1910 by the Japanese gardener Tasa Eida, include an impressive array of plants, from mulberry and cherry trees to magnolias and bamboo. There is a tea house and a miniature village carved out of rock from Mount Fuji. The garden symbolizes the life of a man taking a journey from Birth to Eternity.

Also at Tully House is **St Fiachra's Garden**, a millennium project designed by Martin Hallinan that seeks to re-create a monastic island hermitage in honour of St Fiachra, the patron saint of gardeners. Its use of natural materials, such as rock and water, creates a sense of spirituality and calm. You can see a stone cave decorated in sparkling Waterford Crystal and the statue of St Fiachra holding a seed standing on a rock in the lake.

DID YOU KNOW?

The Japanese Garden at the Kildare Stud, considered the finest Japanese garden in Europe, symbolizes the journey of a soul from birth to eternity, finally coming to rest in the Garden of Peace and Contentment. Along the way the soul encounters the Hill of Learning, the Walk of Wisdom, the Hill of Ambition and the Bridge of Life.

*The fine detail of
Muiredach's Cross,
Monasterboice (left)*

MONASTERBOICE ✪✪

The ruins of the monastery of St Buite, one of the most famous monastic settlements in Ireland, lie in an attractive secluded spot north of Drogheda. Founded in the 6th century, the monastery remained at the height of importance for 600 years until it was superseded by the new Cistercian foundation, Mellifont Abbey. Highlights of the site are the remarkable 10th-century roofless round tower, standing 33m (108ft) high, and the wonderful set of three high crosses. The finest is Muiredach's Cross, with elaborate sculptural detail and an inscription that reads 'A prayer for Muiredach by whom was made this cross'.

 77E5
⊠ Near Drogheda, Co Louth
⊙ Always accessible
🚌 Bus Éireann service 100 to Monsterboice Inn
♿ Few
👆 Free

POWERSCOURT HOUSE AND GARDENS ✪✪✪

Set amid the wild landscape of the Wicklow Mountains, Powerscourt is one of the most magnificent gardens, both formal and semi-natural, in Europe. The view from the terrace is unbeatable, with its sweeping vista and a backdrop of mountain peaks. The original house, built in the 1740s, was gutted by fire in 1974 and has been the subject of a careful restoration project. It now houses an exhibition on the history of Powerscourt. You can visit the former ballroom, and there is a gallery of craft and design shops and a terrace restaurant. But it is for the gardens that most visitors come; laid out in the mid-18th century, they comprise great formal terraces that drop down towards lakes and fountains, statues and decorative ironwork. There are American, Japanese and Italian gardens, as well as charming walled gardens with rose beds and borders, and even a pets' cemetery. The leaflet provided will give you a self-guided tour of the gardens, or you can take a formal tour. If time allows, check out the 121m (397ft) high waterfall, Ireland's highest, 5km (3 miles) away but still on the Powerscourt Estate (summer 9:30–dusk, winter 10:30–dusk, moderate).

www.powerscourt.ie
✚ 77F2
⊠ Powerscourt Estate, Enniskerry, Co Wicklow
☎ 204 6000
⊙ Daily 9:30–5:30. Waterfall: summer until 7pm; winter open from 10:30–dusk
🍴 Restaurant and café (€–€€)
🚌 44
🚆 Bray, then 185 bus
♿ House and some parts of garden good
👆 Expensive for house and gardens, free to enter estate
❓ Guided tour lasts 40 min. Garden centre on site

Trim Castle (below right) was built in the 12th century

SLANE

Despite suffering from heavy traffic congestion, the estate village of Slane is a pleasant place to visit, with its fine Georgian houses. To escape from the busy main street head up the winding lane to the Hill of Slane. From this spot, with its fine views over the surrounding countryside, St Patrick is said to have lit a fire announcing the arrival of Christianity and heralding the end of the pagan Kings of Tara. Here are the remains of a church and college established in 1512. **Slane Castle**, to the west of the village, has been home to the Conynham family since the 18th century. The castle suffered a devastating fire in 1991 and after ten years of renovation reopened to the public in 2001. You can see the fine Gothic Ballroom with its beautiful plasterwork ceiling completed for the visit of George IV in 1821. The grounds of the castle were landscaped by Capability Brown. Now mostly used for conferences, weddings and concerts, Slane Castle has also served as a location for several films and U2 recorded their album, *The Unforgettable Fire*, here in 1984.

TRIM

Trim is a thriving town on the River Boyne, and was once the site of one of the oldest and largest religious settlements in Ireland. The town is dominated by the Anglo-Norman **Trim Castle**, which was built by Hugh de Lacy in 1173. It is the largest such castle in Ireland, enclosing a 1.2ha (3-acre) site. The castle has hardly been altered since the 13th century and still bears the scars of warfare. Visitors can access the 21m (69ft) high keep and grounds on a guided tour. Scenes from the 1995 epic film

An aerial view of the fortifications of Slane Castle (left)

Braveheart were shot here. Across the Boyne are the ruins of Sheep's Gate and the Yellow Steeple – the belfry tower of the former St Mary's Augustinian Abbey dating from 1368 and the most prominent remains here. It rises dramatically from the quiet meadow, left undisturbed since the town developed on the opposite bank in the 18th century. Other ruins of note are the 13th-century Cathedral of St Peter and St Paul and the Hospital of John the Baptist. The visitor centre gives more insight into these medieval ruins in its exhibition, The Power and the Glory, a clever multimedia display that underlines the consequences of the Norman arrival in Ireland.

WICKLOW MOUNTAINS NATIONAL PARK ✪✪✪

A dramatic, secluded area of high mountains, peaceful valleys and lakes on the doorstep of Dublin, this park covers some 20,000ha (49,420 acres) with Lugnaquilla its highest point at 943m (3,094ft). Two scenic passes cross the mountains from east to west – the Sally Gap on the spectacular old military road from Dublin to Laragh, and the Wicklow Gap to the south. Much of the lower mountain slopes are covered in woodland; some trees are believed to be old enough to have supplied the timber for Dublin's St Patrick's Cathedral and London's Palace of Westminster. In the western foothills, several valleys have been flooded to form the Poulaphouca Reservoir, also known as Blessington Lake. This reservoir provides Dublin with water and electricity, and you can take a boat trip on the water. Scattered throughout the park are reminders of ancient settlements – hillforts and stone circles, as well as monastic sites such as Glendalough (► 83), which is where the park information centre is located. Also within the park is Powerscourt House and Gardens (► 87). The area is rich in wildlife and makes for spectacular walking country.

Walking along the Wicklow Way in the Wicklow Mountains (below)

🕂 77E2

🚌 Glendalough bus twice daily from Dublin and Bray

Information Point

✉ Upper Lough, Glendalough, Wicklow Mountains National Park, Co Wicklow

☎ 0404 45425

🕐 May–Sep, daily 10–6; Oct–Apr, weekends 10–dusk

🎟 Free

DID YOU KNOW?

The 132km (82-mile) Wicklow Way, founded in 1963, stretches from Dublin over the Wicklow Mountains to Clonegal in County Carlow and was Ireland's first long-distance walking path. The walk starts in Marlay Park, just outside Dublin, and takes you along forest tracks and country roads to valleys and lakes, and even to the highest village in Ireland, Roundwood.

A Drive Through the Boyne Valley

Distance
162km (100 miles)

Time
A day

Start/end point
Dublin
✚ 77E3

Lunch
Conyngham Arms, Slane
(► 98) or the Ardboyne
Hotel, Navan (► 99)

*Take the N1 north out of Dublin, join the M1
and head north for about 32km (20 miles). Exit
at the junction for Drogheda south and pick up
the N1, then cross the river; turn left onto the
N51. After about 1km (0.6 mile) turn left to the
Boyne battlefield observation area. Pass the car
park and bear right to Donore. Drive through
the village and turn right, following signs for
Brú na Bóinne (► 80).*

This is one of the most important archaeological sites in
Europe and a World Heritage Site.

*Continue along this road until you meet the N2.
Turn right into Slane (► 88). To the west of
the village is Slane Castle. At the crossroads in
Slane turn left along the N51 to Navan. Leave
the town on the N3 south and 6km (4 miles)
after crossing the Boyne again turn right on a
minor road signed to the Hill of Tara (► 85).*

There are wonderful views from the earthworks.

*Head down the hill and turn left at both of the
next junctions, then take the right turn down a
winding minor road. When you come
to a T-junction turn left, then right at
Bective Inn. Cross the bridge and
Bective Abbey (► 78) is on the right,
across the meadows. Continue to the
junction with the R161 and turn left
towards Trim (► 88), with its superb
castle. Take the R158 south out of the
town and carry on through
Summerhill to Kilcock. Pick up the
R148 on the other side of the village, following
the Royal Canal to Maynooth.*

*A herd of cows grazing in
front of Bective Abbey,
County Meath*

Maynooth Castle was home to the Kildare FitzGeralds, one
of the most influential families in Ireland.

*Leaving Maynooth, join the M4 to return to
Dublin.*

Where To...

The rockery garden in the Botanic Gardens (above). A statue of Molly Malone on Lower Grafton Street (right)

Dublin

Prices

Prices are for a three-course meal for one person, excluding wine:
€ = up to €25
€€ = €25–€45
€€€ = over €45

Establishments are open daily unless otherwise stated.

Eating out in Dublin

It can be very expensive to eat out in Dublin and it pays to take advantage of the increasing number of set menus on offer – they may be more limiting than the à la carte but will save you a considerable amount of money. Another option that will not break the bank is the early-bird menu, mostly available in mid-range restaurants. You can have two or three courses for almost half price providing you eat before 7pm..

AYA (€€)

A hip Japanese sushi bar furnished with minimalist wooden tables and chairs. Help yourself to the many delicacies as they glide past on the revolving conveyor belt. There is seating for normal dining, too.

✉ **Brown's Department Store, Clarendon Street** ☎ 677 1544 ◎ **Lunch, dinner** 🚉 **Pearse** 🚌 **Cross-city buses**

Bad Ass Café (€€)

Bad Ass Café sticks to what it's best at – good-value pizza, burgers and salad. Artists, musicians and students are attracted by the convivial atmosphere. An ingenious pulley system still partly in operation whisks your order overhead to the kitchen.

✉ **9–11 Crown Alley** ☎ 671 2596 ◎ **Lunch, dinner** 🚉 **Tara Street** 🚌 **Cross-city buses**

Bang Café (€€)

A hip clientele comes here for the buzz and the modern European menu that is as cool and trendy as the interior. Try the Thai noodles or bangers and mash. Friendly staff.

✉ **11 Merrion Row** ☎ 676 0898 ◎ **Lunch, dinner. Closed Sun** 🚉 **Pearse** 🚌 **Cross-city buses**

Bewley's Oriental Café (€)

Steeped in history and folklore, Bewley's glorious wooden panelled rooms with stained-glass windows make the perfect place to relax over a cup of tea or coffee, sample the cakes and sticky buns or enjoy a hearty breakfast. There's another branch at Westmoreland Street.

✉ **78–79 Grafton Street** ☎ 635 5470 ◎ **Breakfast, lunch, dinner** 🚉 **Pearse** 🚌 **Cross-city buses**

Botticelli (€€)

Authentic Italian restaurant serving dependable traditional cuisine – pizza, pasta, fish and chicken dishes, and mouth-watering desserts – in welcoming surroundings. If you book early you can get a table overlooking the river.

✉ **3 Temple Bar** ☎ 672 7289 ◎ **Lunch, dinner** 🚉 **Tara Street** 🚌 **Cross-city buses**

Brazen Head (€€)

Reputed to be the oldest bar in town, the Brazen Head has loads of old-world charm. The first-floor restaurant, with large dressers and stucco ceilings, offers Californian and modern Irish cooking. Downstairs a carvery is served at lunchtime.

✉ **20 Bridge Street Lower** ☎ 679 5186 ◎ **Lunch, dinner** 🚌 **51B, 78A**

Brownes Brasserie (€€€)

A sophisticated dining-room with chandeliers housed in a Georgian town-house hotel facing on to St Stephen's Green. The classy fare is Continental, with the emphasis on seafood; try the monkfish wrapped in *pancetta*.

✉ **22 St Stephen's Green North** ☎ 638 3939 ◎ **Lunch Sun–Fri, dinner daily** 🚉 **Pearse** 🚌 **Cross-city buses**

Bruno's (€€)

A modern hot-spot that serves a fusion of European and French dishes such as *boudin* of crab with *velouté* of basil, or guinea fowl with cep risotto. Bruno's has now added a jazz bar (Fri–Sat only) for more casual dining while listening to music.

✉ **21 Kildare Street** ☎ **662 4724** ⊙ **Lunch Mon–Fri, dinner Tue–Sat** 🚉 **Tara Street** 🚌 **Cross-city buses**

Café Java (€)
A popular breakfast and lunchtime haunt catering to all tastes – from bagels and wraps to chicken with yogurt or poached eggs with bacon. You may have to wait but newspapers are on hand

✉ **5 Anne Street South** ☎ **670 7239** ⊙ **Breakfast, lunch** 🚉 **Pearse** 🚌 **Cross-city buses**

Café Mao (€€)
This slick place, decorated with Warhol posters, attracts a young clientele. Delicious Oriental dishes like grilled, marinated squid with watermelon or Malaysian chicken are excellent.

✉ **2–3 Chatham Row** ☎ **670 4899** ⊙ **Lunch, dinner** 🚉 **Pearse** 🚌 **Cross-city buses**

Cavistons (€€)
Sandycove is justifiably proud of its small seafood restaurant that serves wonderfully fresh, simply cooked fish that speaks for itself. Very popular so book well in advance.

✉ **59 Glasthule Road, Sandycove** ☎ **280 9245** ⊙ **Three sittings: noon–1:30, 1:30–3 or 3–5. Closed Sun and Mon** 🚉 **Sandycove/Glasthule** 🚌 **59**

Cedar Tree (€€)
A delicious selection of Lebanese dishes and *meze* (falafel, spicy sausage) is offered up in a Middle Eastern ambience. Saturday evening gets lively with traditional music and a belly dancer to entertain.

✉ **11 St Andrew's Street** ☎ **677 2121** ⊙ **Dinner only** 🚉 **Pearse** 🚌 **Cross-city buses**

Chapter One (€€)
In the basement beneath the Dublin Writers Museum, the dining-room has pictures of Irish writers on the wall. Organic produce is used in top-notch modern Irish cooking. Seared scallops and fennel, and roast venison are among delights on the menu, but it changes regularly.

✉ **18–19 Parnell Square** ☎ **873 2266** ⊙ **Closed Sun–Mon** 🚉 **Connolly** 🚌 **Cross-city buses**

Chilli Club (€€)
The longest-serving Thai restaurant in Dublin is still respected for its tasty – and hot – curries and satays at reasonable prices. Cosy dining-room.

✉ **1 Anne's Lane, off Anne Street South** ☎ **677 3721** ⊙ **Lunch Mon–Sat, dinner daily** 🚉 **Pearse** 🚌 **Cross-city buses**

Cobalt Café (€)
An ideal spot for a quick snack; the light menu at this bright and airy café offers generously filled sandwiches and cakes. Arty types come here to see the display of original paintings on the walls.

✉ **16 North Great George's Street** ☎ **873 0313** ⊙ **Mon–Sat 10–4:30. Closed Sun** 🚉 **Connolly** 🚌 **Cross-city buses**

Cooke's Café (€€)
A fashionable spot with a Mediterranean atmosphere, popular with celebrities. Californian cuisine with Italian influences features on the comprehensive menu; grilled gambas or the mussels always go down well. An outside terrace is used for summer dining.

✉ **14 William Street South** ☎ **679 0536** ⊙ **Lunch, dinner. Closed Sun, Mon dinner** 🚉 **Pearse** 🚌 **Cross-city buses**

What's What
Dining out is one of the most popular pastimes in Dublin, so it's advisable to book ahead if you have your mind set on a particular establishment; check opening hours as some places close on Monday or Sunday. Many restaurants add a service charge of 12.5 per cent to the bill but if they don't, a tip of 10–15 per cent is the norm. Several restaurants offer a fixed-price lunch menu, which is excellent value.

Pub Food

Pub grub is increasingly popular in Dublin and the hearty, substantial food offered is generally good value. Some of the pubs that have become tourist attractions have slightly inflated prices, and you can pay more for the added attraction of live music. Eating in a pub gives you the chance to sample more of the local dishes like Irish stews and colcannon (cabbage and potato), and there is often a carvery available. Good grub, a pint of Guinness, Irish music and a great atmosphere – what more could you want?

Cornucopia (€)

Established, buffet-style vegetarian restaurant that provides healthy and wholesome food. The hot breakfast is a must, and the casseroles and vegetable quiches are good, too.

🖂 19 Wicklow Street 🕿 677 7583 🕔 Breakfast, lunch, dinner Mon–Sat (Sun till 7) 🚊 Pearse 🚌 Cross-city buses

Dunne & Crescenzi (€)

An Italian deli and wine shop that has moved more towards its café operation. The freshest deli-type dishes, such as authentic paninis made with buffalo mozzarella, are served on individual wooden platters.

🖂 14 Frederick Street South 🕿 675 9892 🕔 Lunch, dinner. Closed Sun 🚊 Pearse 🚌 Cross-city buses

Eden (€€)

Modern Irish cuisine with a Mediterranean twist is served in a chic, stark white interior with huge picture windows. Dishes such as blackened salmon or braised lamb steaks with olives and lemon barley are memorable. On summer evenings, when Temple Bar is in full swing, tables spill on to the lively square.

🖂 Meeting House Square 🕿 670 5372 🕔 Lunch, dinner 🚊 Tara Street 🚌 Cross-city buses

Fadó (€€€)

Next to the Lord Mayor's residence, this spacious, belle-époque dining-room offers superb contemporary Irish cuisine with international touches, served by charming staff.

🖂 The Mansion House, Dawson Street 🕿 676 7200 🕔 Lunch, dinner. Closed Sun 🚊 Pearse 🚌 Cross-city buses

Fitzer's (€€)

A popular restaurant chain offering relaxed dining. This one is a bright high-tech space with a fiery modern European menu. There is another branch at the National Gallery.

🖂 51 Dawson Street 🕿 677 1155 🕔 Lunch, dinner 🚊 Pearse 🚌 Cross-city buses

Gallagher's Boxty House (€€)

Something you don't very often get in Dublin these days – real Irish food, focused around boxty, the Irish potato pancake. The great atmosphere and country-style setting – and the food of course – are popular with visitors.

🖂 20–21 Temple Bar 🕿 677 2762 🕔 Lunch, dinner 🚊 Tara Street 🚌 Cross-city buses

Good World Restaurant (€€)

Dublin Chinese residents come here themselves to eat superb Chinese food. It is considered by many to have the best dim sum in Dublin. Open late.

🖂 18 South Great George's Street 🕿 677 5373 🕔 Lunch, dinner 🚊 Tara Street 🚌 Cross-city buses

Gotham Café (€)

A young crowd gathers at this vibrant haunt with a Manhattan theme to enjoy delicious pizza. Rolling Stones' album covers are plastered all over the walls. Always busy so book ahead.

🖂 8 Anne Street South 🕿 679 5266 🕔 Lunch, dinner 🚊 Pearse 🚌 Cross-city buses

Guinea Pig Fish Restaurant (€€€)

Just down the hill from the Dalkey DART station, this family-run restaurant offers fairly traditional seafood-based dishes. Brass ornaments and china plates give it a rustic feel.

✉ **17 Railway Road, Dalkey**
☎ **285 9055** 🕐 **Dinner only**
🚉 **Dalkey** 🚌 **59**

Halo (€€€€)

Minimalist in style, this chic restaurant is in a striking atrium setting. The Irish/Asian fusion cooking includes divine dishes along the lines of chorizo red pepper stew and spiced monkfish, all presented with flair.

✉ **Morrison Hotel, Ormond Quay Lower** ☎ **887 2421**
🕐 **Breakfast, dinner and Sun brunch** 🚉 **Tara Street**
🚌 **Cross-city buses**

Il Baccaro (€€)

Rustic trattoria set in the vaulted chambers of a cellar where a great atmosphere prevails. Authentic Italian food and fine Italian wines straight from barrel.

✉ **Diceman's Corner, Meeting House Square** ☎ **671 4597**
🕐 **Dinner daily, lunch Sat only**
🚉 **Tara Street** 🚌 **Cross-city buses**

Jacob's Ladder (€€)

Formal restaurant with lovely views over the Trinity College playing fields. The imaginative modern Irish cuisine has a style of its own and is some of the best in Dublin.

✉ **4–5 Nassau Street** ☎ **670 3865** 🕐 **Closed Sun, Mon**
🚉 **Pearse** 🚌 **Cross-city buses**

Juice (€)

Cool place for cool people looking for a healthy option. Mostly dedicated to juices and smoothies, and vegetarian food inspired by cuisine from Japan to Mexico and the Caribbean.

✉ **73–83 South Great George's Street** ☎ **475 7856** 🕐 **Lunch, dinner** 🚉 **Tara Street** 🚌 **Cross-city buses**

Kelly and Ping (€€)

There is a cheery atmosphere at this excellent fusion eatery where bonsai trees, huge buddhas and colourful murals complete the scene. The menu has all the normal Oriental classics, as well as tasty specials like Thai marinated sirloin.

✉ **Smithfield Village** ☎ **817 3840** 🕐 **Lunch, dinner**
🚉 **Smithfield LUAS** 🚌 **83**

King Stiric's (€€€€)

Dine on exquisite fresh seafood caught at the nearby pier in this restaurant while enjoying stirring sea views. The weekday set lunch is good value.

✉ **East Pier, Howth** ☎ **832 5235**
🕐 **Lunch Mon–Fri, dinner Mon–Sat** 🚉 **Howth** 🚌 **31, 31B**

La Stampa (€€€)

Dine on superb modern European cooking, which delivers such treats as *sevruga* caviar followed by roast monk fish tail with *pepperonata* and Serrano ham, in a 19th-century ballroom adorned with rich fabrics, mirrors, fine artwork and candles.

✉ **35 Dawson Street** ☎ **677 8611** 🕐 **Dinner only. Closed Sun** 🚉 **Pearse** 🚌 **Cross-city buses**

L'Ecrivain (€€€)

Portraits of Irish writers decorate the walls of the sparkling dining-room, where chef Derry Clarke conjures up his French-inspired modern Irish cuisine. Heavenly dishes are complemented by excellent wines. Very expensive but worth every penny.

✉ **109a Baggot Street Lower**
☎ **661 1919** 🕐 **Lunch Mon–Fri, dinner Mon–Sat** 🚌 **10A**

Fish for Dinner

Fresh fish and seafood is plentiful in Dublin and the city prides itself on having some of the best fish restaurants around. Oysters, mussels, crab, prawns, salmon, ray, mackerel, sole, whiting and trout are all found in the local waters. In Ireland, Monday is not a good day to eat fresh fish as the fishermen take a rest on Sunday and there are no deliveries the following day, so the choice is limited. Most surprisingly with all this fresh fish and seafood available, it doesn't come cheap.

World Cuisines

In Dublin today the selection of restaurants offering dishes from around the world is vast. The options range from French, Italian and Mediterranean cooking to the more exotic tastes from Mexico, India, China, Japan and Southeast Asia (especially Thai), and you can also enjoy Russian and Lebanese fare..

Les Frères Jacques (€€€)

The emphasis at this stylish restaurant is on fish and seafood, but there are also delicious meat options on the menu. Efficient and courteous staff.

⊠ 74 Dame Street ☎ 679 4555 ◎ Lunch Mon–Fri, dinner Mon–Sat ☒ Tara Street ▣ Cross-city buses

Lobster Pot (€€€)

Delightfully old-fashioned restaurant, with a nautical theme, reminiscent of a gentleman's club. First-class traditional French cooking that specializes in fish. The attentive staff will ensure you have a memorable dining experience.

⊠ 9 Ballsbridge Terrace, Ballsbridge ☎ 668 0025 ◎ Closed Sat Lunch & Sun ☒ Lansdowne Road ▣ 5, 7, 7A, 45

Lord Edward (€€€)

Dublin's oldest seafood restaurant is in traditional surroundings above a pub. Dedicated to simple but very tasty fish dishes and luscious desserts like meringue drizzled with *crème anglaise*.

⊠ 23 Christchurch Place ☎ 454 2420 ◎ Lunch Mon–Fri, dinner Mon–Sat ▣ Cross-city buses

Mermaid Café (€€)

Bright and airy hot spot with unfussy minimalist fittings. An eclectic menu of Irish fare offers tasty fun dishes, but the biggest lure is the house special, crab cakes.

⊠ 69 Dame Street ☎ 670 8236 ◎ Lunch, dinner ☒ Tara Street ▣ Cross-city buses

Monty's of Kathmandu (€€€)

A warm welcome is extended at this Nepalese restaurant with its set menu of creative dishes. Monty's was the winner of Bushmills Malt 'Best Ethnic Restaurant in Dublin' for 2002/2003.

⊠ 28 Eustace Street ☎ 670 4911 ◎ Lunch, dinner. Closed Sun lunch ☒ Tara Street ▣ Cross-city buses

Nude (€)

Eco-friendly café selling mouth-watering healthy options – hot and cold wraps, salads, low-fat organic desserts, fresh fruit and juices – that can be taken away or eaten at the communal tables.

⊠ 21 Suffolk Street ☎ 677 4804 ◎ Lunch , dinner daily (Sun till 7pm) ☒ Pearse ▣ Cross-city buses

Oliver St John Gogarty (€€)

There's a more formal restaurant on the first floor of this traditional Irish pub where you can eat such delights as a vast pot of mussels cooked in wine and Bailey's sauce, or a generous helping of Irish stew. If you prefer things more lively, pub food is served downstairs with live Irish music; the atmosphere is fantastic.

⊠ 58–59 Fleet Street ☎ 671 1822 ◎ Lunch, dinner; Sun dinner only ☒ Tara Street ▣ Cross-city buses

Patrick Guilbaud (€€€)

Beautifully cooked and presented dishes clearly show the flair and innovation of this French chef, said to be the best in Dublin. The elegant dining-room has a fine collection of Irish art and the service is second to none.

⊠ Merrion Hotel, 21 Upper Merrion Street ☎ 676 4192 ◎ Lunch, dinner Tue–Sat ☒ Pearse ▣ Cross-city buses

Queen of Tarts (€)

You'll think you're in heaven when you set eyes on the yummy display of cakes, tarts, cookies and savoury treats at this traditional teashop.

⊠ 4 Cork Hill, Dame Street

☎ 670 7499 ⊚ Daily 🚆 Tara Street 🚌 Cross-city buses

Rajdoot Tandoori (€€€)
Outstanding North Indian food is served in plush surroundings with elaborate friezes on the walls. There's only one sitting so guests will not be rushed by the courteous staff. Good vegetarian options.
✉ Westbury Hotel, Clarendon Street ☎ 679 4274 ⊚ Lunch Mon–Sat, dinner daily
🚆 Pearse 🚌 Cross-city buses

Roly's (€€)
This buzzing bistro is popular with the locals, which makes for a great atmosphere. Robust Irish dishes like pork stuffed with rhubarb and apple have something different and the freshly baked speciality breads alone are worth the trip to Ballsbridge.
✉ 7 Ballsbridge Terrace, Ballsbridge ☎ 668 2611
⊚ Lunch, dinner
🚆 Landsdowne Road 🚌 5, 7, 7A, 45

Shalimar (€€)
A wide variety of innovative dishes from the regions of India served in a large candlelit room with Indian décor. In the basement is a less formal setting offering simple balti dishes.
✉ 17 South Great George's Street ☎ 671 0738 ⊚ Lunch Mon–Fri, dinner daily
🚆 Pearse 🚌 Cross-city buses

Tea Room at the Clarence (€€€)
Inside a prestigious hotel owned by the rock group U2, this is a magnet for Dublin's rich and famous. Exciting modern Irish food is served in a spacious, serene room with soaring ceilings where natural light pours in through huge windows. If you can afford the exorbitant prices, this is a must.

✉ The Clarence, 6–8 Wellington Quay ☎ 670 7766
⊚ Closed Sat lunch 🚆 Tara Street 🚌 Cross-city buses

Thornton's (€€€)
Chef Kevin Thornton's reputation for exquisite cooking is flying high and his restaurant is arguably one of the best in Ireland. The crisp, clean-cut dining-room, with lush brown velvet chairs, boasts innovative international dishes that focus mainly on game and seafood.
✉ Fitzwilliam Hotel, 128 St Stephen's Green ☎ 478 7008
⊚ Closed Sun, Mon 🚆 Pearse 🚌 Cross-city buses

Unicorn (€€€)
Fashionable lunch spot where socialites gather to eat from the antipasto bar. In the evening there's a bistro-style menu of Italian classics served in a plain, unspoilt *trattoria*-style setting.
✉ 12B Merrion Court, off Merrion Row ☎ 676 2182
⊚ Lunch, dinner. Closed Sun 🚌 Cross-city buses

Winding Stair Café (€)
An atmospheric café at the top of a spiral staircase leading from the dusty old bookshop below. Enjoy a fine view of the River Liffey while sipping coffee or enjoying a snack.
✉ 40 Ormond Quay Lower ☎ 873 3292 ⊚ Lunch Mon–Sat
🚆 Tara Street 🚌 Cross-city buses

Yamamori Noodles (€€)
This Japanese noodle and sushi house will never fail to impress. A cheerful and sociable atmosphere plus great food makes for an enjoyable meal.
✉ 71–72 South Great Georges Street ☎ 475 5001 ⊚ Lunch, dinner 🚆 Pearse 🚌 Cross-city buses

Good Start to the Day
More and more restaurants and cafés in Dublin are opening earlier or extending their menus as it becomes evident the number of people eating out first thing in the morning is increasing. A hearty traditional Irish breakfast consists of bacon, sausage, egg, mushrooms, tomato, black and white pudding (sausage-shaped meat product made from cows' blood and served in fried slices), and toast, washed down with strong tea or coffee.

Around Dublin

Avoca Cafés

The Avoca Handweavers (▶ 78), founded in 1723, have added award-winning cafés to their business empire. There are branches around the Dublin area at Kilmacanoge (▶ 99), Avoca Village, Powerscourt House (▶ 99) and Suffolk Street (▶ 104) in the city centre. Famous for their home-made products, Avoca's innovative menus include Thai broth, confit of duck salad, beef stew and a selection of breads with various dips. They are legendary for their desserts and their excellent scones and biscuits. Look out for *The Avoca Café Cookbook* on sale in their shops.

Co Dublin
Johnnie Fox's Pub (€)
Beams and an open fire set the scene at this 18th-century coaching inn, a local legend known for its superb seafood, especially the fresh mussels. Traditional music sessions are held nightly.
🖂 **Glencullen** ☎ **295 5647**

Co Kildare
Ballymore Inn (€€)
People come from miles around to this country pub to enjoy the superb food: pizzas and open sandwiches, salads and pasta dishes. The informal dining area has an open fire and fresh flowers.
🖂 **Ballymore Eustace** ☎ **045 864 585** 🍴 **Closed Sun, Mon dinner (Mon lunch & Sun bar food only)**

Byerley Turk (€€€)
A sumptuous hotel restaurant with high ceilings, chandeliers, lavish drapes and fine views of the hotel gardens. French cuisine with an Irish slant uses vegetables and fruit from the hotel's garden.
🖂 **Kildare Hotel and Golf Club, Straffan** ☎ **601 7200** 🍴 **Dinner only**

High Cross Inn (€)
Delightful roadside pub dating back to the 1870s, containing lots of interesting old artefacts and open fires; sheep roam freely outside. The inn has gained a reputation for its excellent traditional dishes.
🖂 **Bolton Hill, Moone** ☎ **05986 24112** 🍴 **Lunch, dinner**

Leixlip House (€€)
Accomplished modern Irish cooking with an occasional Mediterranean twist is served in the bright, elegant dining-room of this country hotel. Fixed-price set menu.
🖂 **Captains Hill, Leixlip** ☎ **624 2268** 🍴 **Closed lunch Tue–Sat**

Michelangelo Restaurant (€)
This family-run Irish–Italian restaurant, just outside the gates of Castletown House, has been here for over 20 years. Serving home-style Italian fare it is renowed for its prawn and sole dishes.
🖂 **Main Street, Celbridge** ☎ **627 1809** 🍴 **Dinner Tue-Sun, lunch Sun only**

Moyglare Manor (€€€)
The candlelit dining-room is a romantic setting to enjoy imaginative food prepared using fruit and vegetables from the hotel's gardens. Crab claws and prawns on a potato gallette might be followed by baked fillet of turbot with an aromatic cream and bay leaf sauce.
🖂 **Maynooth** ☎ **628 6351** 🍴 **Closed lunch Sat**

Turner Restaurant (€€€)
Gracious columned restaurant decked out in scarlet and gold, with high ceilings and chandeliers, serving excellent Irish and Mediterranean options. A harpist entertains on Friday and Saturday evenings.
🖂 **Killashee House Hotel, Naas** ☎ **045 879 277** 🍴 **Dinner, Lunch on Sun only**

Co Louth
Forge Gallery Restaurant (€€€)
This hospitable restaurant, decorated with flair, is a great setting for excellent food combining rustic French, New Irish and world

cuisines. The home-made breads are delicious.

✉ **Collon** ☎ 041 982 6272
🕐 Dinner only Tue–Sat

Jordan's Townhouse Restaurant (€€)

In a lovely setting overlooking the harbour, it's hardly surprising that this former 17th-century fisherman's cottage specializes in fresh seafood.

✉ **Newry Street, Carlingford** ☎ 042 937 3223 🕐 Dinner only

Co Meath
Conyngham Arms (€)

This old-world village inn behind an attractive stone façade makes a great pitstop when touring the beautiful Boyne Valley. Lunch is served in the Blackbird Carvery and dinner in the Gamekeeper's Lodge Bistro.

✉ **Slane** ☎ 041 988 4444
🕐 Lunch, dinner

The Ardboyne (€€)

A warm and comfortable atmosphere prevails at this friendly hotel, where the restaurant overlooks pretty gardens. The evening à la carte or set menu offers a variety of modern Irish-inspired dishes and the lunchtime carvery makes this an ideal midday stop-off.

✉ **Ardboyne Hotel, Dublin Road, Navan** ☎ 046 902 3119
🕐 Lunch, dinner

Co Wicklow
Avoca Handweavers (€)

A simple restaurant selling Avoca's tried and tested home-cooked food and delicious lunches based on organic and locally produced ingredients – farmhouse cheeses, home-baked breads and preserves.

✉ **Avoca Mill, Kilmacanoge, near Bray** ☎ 286 7466
🕐 Lunch only

Downshire House (€€€€)

Relax in comfortable surroundings amid Georgian décor while dining on fine uncomplicated local and international cuisine. The menu includes such dishes as roast stuffed leg of Wicklow lamb with mint sauce and baked fillet of sea trout with toasted almonds.

✉ **Blessington** ☎ 045 865 199
🕐 Lunch, dinner

Hungry Monk (€€€)

Small, intimate restaurant where candlelit tables set the scene, in a lovely position overlooking a golf course. The unpretentious, changing menu has traditional Irish dishes; duck always features.

✉ **Church Road, Greystones** ☎ 287 5759 🕐 Dinner Wed–Sat, lunch Sun only

Hunter's Hotel (€€€)

Admire the beautiful gardens of this country-house hotel through the dining-room windows as you eat from a stylish menu of tasty meat and fish dishes.

✉ **Rathnew** ☎ 0404 40106
🕐 Lunch, dinner

Powerscourt Terrace Café (€)

The ideal spot for panoramic views of the gardens against the backdrop of the Wicklow Mountains. The Terrace Café offers first-class fare from the Avoca cookbook.

✉ **Powerscourt House, Enniskerry** ☎ 204 6070
🕐 Lunch only

Roundwood Inn (€€)

Cosy inn – popular with hikers walking the Wicklow Mountains – complete with roaring log fires and wooden benches. The award-winning food, specializing in seafood and game, is served in the bar and in the restaurant.

✉ **Main Street, Roundwood** ☎ 281 8107 🕐 Bar meals daily; restaurant dinner Fri, Sat (more evenings when busy)

Traditional Irish

Simplicity is the key when it comes to good Irish cooking, using fresh local produce. There are more and more culinary trendsetters arriving on the scene, but many restaurants still adopt a traditional style, serving seafood chowder, smoked salmon and hearty soups and stews accompanied by soda bread (a yeast-free loaf), in settings with log fires and local music. One of the most popular images of Irish cuisine is a plate of oysters and a pint of Guinness, truly food of the gods.

Dublin

Prices

The price indications below are for a double room per night:

€ = under €100
€€ = €100–€200
€€€ = over €200

Staying in Dublin

Dublin room rates fluctuate throughout the year, peaking from June through to September, over public holidays or during special events. The choice of accommodation ranges from luxury hotels to self-catering hostels. Rooms in Dublin are not cheap in comparison to some European cities, although with so much competition between hotels there are special offers to be had. Rates normally include full Irish breakfast, service charge and VAT (currently 21 per cent) but it's best to check when making your reservation.

Aston Hotel (€)

At the top end of this category, Aston Hotel provides a haven in contrast to the buzz of Temple Bar outside. Simple rooms with good use of pastel shades and pine furniture have a modern airy feel.

www.aston-hotel.com ⊠ 7–9 Aston Quay ☎ 677 9300; fax 677 9007 🚉 Tara Street 🚌 Cross-city buses

Barnacles Temple Bar House (€)

Superior budget accommodation with en-suite bedrooms, many overlooking the cobbled streets of Temple Bar. Communal TV room, self-catering facilities and breakfast room.

www.barnacles.ie ⊠ 19 Temple Lane South ☎ 671 6277; fax 671 6591 🚉 Tara Street 🚌 Cross-city buses

Clarence (€€€)

Originally built in 1852, U2's Bono and The Edge have brought a fabulous contemporary look to this classic hotel in Temple Bar. The chic interior has soft suede and leather and stunning floral arrangements. Individually designed guest rooms are stylishly decorated with rich colours and have crisp white linen.

www.theclarence.ie ⊠ 6–8 Wellington Quay ☎ 407 0800; fax 407 0820 🚉 Tara Street 🚌 Cross-city buses

Grafton Capital (€€)

Traditional Georgian town house well placed for Grafton Street and Dublin's cultural area. Modern spacious bedrooms are tastefully decorated and well equipped. Very friendly staff. Adjoining bar and restaurant.

www.capital-hotels.com ⊠ Stephen's Street Lower ☎ 648 1100; fax 648 1122 🚉 Pearse 🚌 Cross-city buses

Gresham (€€€)

A central landmark, Dublin's oldest hotel underwent a major transformation in 2000 to provide a bright, more modern look – but the attentive staff remain the same. Huge bedrooms combine traditional style with modern comfort.

www.gresham-hotels.com ⊠ Upper O'Connell Street ☎ 874 6881; fax 878 7171 🚉 Connolly 🚌 Cross-city buses

Harding (€)

Close to Temple Bar, opposite Christ Church Cathedral. Roomy en-suite bedrooms furnished in pine have bright and cheery soft furnishings and most modern facilities. The lively bar and restaurant has music on some evenings.

www.hardinghotel.ie ⊠ Copper Alley, Fishamble Street ☎ 679 6500; fax 679 6504 🚌 Cross-city buses

Harrington Hall (€€)

This beautifully restored Georgian guest-house beside St Stephen's Green offers the personal touch. Original Georgian features have been retained, coupled with all modern facilities. Generously proportioned bedrooms are furnished with elegant dark wood.

www.harringtonhall.com ⊠ 70 Harcourt Street ☎ 475 3497; fax 475 4544 🚌 Cross-city buses

Jurys Inn Christchurch (€€)

Good-value, modern, central hotel opposite Christ Church Cathedral and a short stroll from Temple Bar. Spacious, well-appointed rooms can accommodate up to three adults and two children. Coffee bar, restaurant and adjoining car park.
www.bookajurysinn.com
✉ Christchurch Place ☎ 607 0000; fax 631 0012 🚌 Cross-city buses

Merrion (€€€)

The Merrion is the epitome of grandeur in the heart of Georgian Dublin. Inviting bedrooms are decorated in classic styles that reflect the 18th-century architecture and have opulent marble bathrooms. Renowned for its restaurant, Patrick Guilbaud (► 96),. Pool, gym and spa.
www.merrionhotel.com
✉ Merrion Street Upper ☎ 603 0600; fax 603 0700 🚇 Pearse 🚌 Cross-city buses

Mespil (€€)

A warm and friendly welcome greets you at this modern hotel overlooking the Grand Canal. Stylish bedrooms offer a high level of comfort at good prices.
www.leehotels.com ✉ Mespil Road ☎ 667 1222; fax 667 1244 🚇 Grand Canal Dock 🚌 11,11A, 11B, 13B, 46A, 46B

Morgan (€€)

A contemporary design based on uncluttered elegance, with clean simple lines. Eye-catching bedrooms feature beechwood furniture, crisp cotton sheets and spacious bathrooms, and superior facilities include ISDN lines, VCRs and CD players. On the edge of Temple Bar.
www.themorgan.com ✉ 10 Fleet Street ☎ 679 3939; fax 679 3946 🚇 Tara Street 🚌 Cross-city buses

Morrison (€€€)

Wood, stone and natural fabrics combine with vibrant colours to create a luxurious feel at this visually stunning boutique hotel created by Irish designer John Rocha. Bedrooms are equipped with all mod cons. Overlooking the River Liffey.
www.morrisonhotel.ie
✉ Lower Ormond Quay ☎ 887 2400; fax 874 4039 🚇 Tara Street 🚌 Cross-city buses

Pembroke Townhouse (€€)

Excellent accommodation and service has won this 18th-century town house in Ballsbridge a loyal following. Individually decorated bedrooms merge modern style with Georgian elegance, and feature contemporary Irish art on the walls.
www.pembroketownhouse.ie
✉ 90 Pembroke Road ☎ 660 0277; fax 660 0291 🚇 Lansdowne Road 🚌 5, 7, 7A, 10A

Shelbourne Le Méridien (€€€)

Founded in 1824, this much-loved hotel has a rich and historic past. The graceful Georgian building has retained its endearing grandeur and boasts a stylish address overlooking St Stephen's Green.
www.shelbourne.ie ✉ 27 St Stephen's Green ☎ 663 4500; fax 661 6006 🚇 Pearse 🚌 Cross-city buses

Staunton on the Green (€€)

Large Georgian house in a delightful position overlooking St Stephen's Green and adjoining the Iveagh Gardens. The spacious bedrooms are decorated in warm shades and all have excellent views.
www.stauntonsonthegreen.ie
✉ 83 St Stephen's Green ☎ 478 2300; fax 478 2263 🚇 Pearse 🚌 Cross-city buses

Availability

It is always best to reserve a room before arriving in Dublin. Accommodation levels in the city have risen considerably since the mid-1990s but the demand has increased equally and it can be difficult to find rooms at busy times. Many hotels will no longer take large groups, having been discouraged by the stag and hen parties that have plagued the city.

Around Dublin

Golf Hotels
The Kildare Hotel (see this page) has been chosen to host the Ryder Cup in 2006, a move guaranteed to boost the popularity of golf and double the demand for golf hotels in the area. Hotels that already satisfy this need include:

Deer Park Hotel & Golf Courses
On a quiet hillside overlooking the sea, this fine hotel complex features five courses.
www.deerpark-hotel.ie
🚩 Howth ☎ 832 2624; fax 839 2405

Portmarnock Hotel & Golf Links
Comfort, good food and world-class golf in one package at this established hotel close to Dublin airport.
www.portmarnock.com
🚩 Strand Road, Portmarnock ☎ 846 0611; fax 846 2442

Co Kildare
Hazel Hotel (€€)
Modern motel-style accommodation in the picturesque town of Monasterevin, close to the Japanese Gardens and Curragh Racecourse. The comfortable en-suite rooms are decorated with bright modern fabrics.
www.hazelhotel.com ✉ Dublin Road, Monasterevin ☎ 045 525 373; fax 045 525 810

Kildare Hotel and Golf Club (€€)
This luxurious hotel beside the River Liffey upholds the highest standards. Gracious, individually furnished rooms offer lavish and refined comfort, and all have views over the gardens and river or the golf course. Byerley Turk restaurant (▶ 98).
www.kclub.ie ✉ Straffan ☎ 601 7200; fax 601 7299

Killashee House (€€€)
Amid exquisite gardens and woodland, with magnificent views of the Wicklow Mountains, this majestic Victorian manor house is steeped in history and has elegant rooms decorated with antiques and warm colours. Spa facilities. Turner Restaurant (▶ 000).
www.killasheehouse.com ✉ Killashee Demesne, Naas ☎ 045 879 277; fax 045 879 266

Moyglare Manor (€€€)
A tree-lined avenue leads to this 18th-century stone house filled with antiques and set in lovely grounds surrounded by country landscape and mature woodlands. Elegant rooms with period furniture – some with four posters – and delicate fabrics have a true country ambience. Restaurant (▶ 98).
www.moyglaremanor.ie ✉ Maynooth ☎ 628 6351; fax 628 5405

Co Louth
Bellingham Castle Hotel (€€)
On the coast, in wonderful surroundings, this 17th-century castle oozes old-world splendour. Modern facilities harmonize with antiques and all rooms – decorated with bright hues – have breathtaking views.
www.bellinghamcastle.com ✉ Castlebellingham ☎ 042 937 2176; fax 042 937 2766

Boyne Valley Hotel & Country Club (€€)
A gracious building in the Boyne Valley surrounded by gardens and woodlands. In the large bedrooms pastel shades, floral fabrics and darkwood furniture give a country feel. Leisure facilities include a swimming pool, beauty clinic and tennis.
www.boyne-valley-hotel.ie ✉ Stameen, Dublin Road, Drogheda ☎ 041 983 7737; fax 041 983 9188

Carrickdale Hotel (€€)
Large modern hotel in landscaped gardens with extensive health and leisure facilities. The bedrooms are contemporary and have modern facilities. Restaurant and nightclub.
www.carrickdale.com ✉ Carrickcarnon, Dundalk ☎ 042 937 1397; fax 042 937 1740

McKevitt's Village Hotel (€€)
Resembling a village pub from the outside, inside is a

modernized hotel that provides a high standard of comfort with simply furnished bedrooms, all en-suite, and modern facilities. On the Cooley Peninsula.
www.mckevittshotel.com
✉ **Market Square, Carlingford** ☎ **042 937 3116; fax 042 937 3144**

Co Meath
Annesbrook (€€)
In a tranquil spot in the heart of the Boyne Valley, Annesbrook has a lovely walled garden and orchard that keep the kitchen supplied with fresh fruit and vegetables. The charming rooms have Victorian-style fittings and furniture.
www.annesbrook.com
✉ **Duleek** ☎ **041 982 3293; fax 041 982 3024**

Ashbourne House Hotel (€€)
Starting out in 1850 as a coach stop, this refurbished hotel offers a fine blend of traditional and contemporary design in relaxing surroundings. Eating options include a carvery and the excellent Loft restaurant.
www.ashbournehousehotel.com
✉ **Main Street, Ashbourne** ☎ **835 8400; fax 835 8424**

Conyngham Arms Hotel (€€)
In the heart of the picturesque village of Slane, this mid-19th-century building has a distinctive stone façade. The cosy inside is Victorian in style with four-poster beds. Restaurant (▶ 99).
www.conynghamarms.com
✉ **Slane** ☎ **041 988 4444**

Station House Hotel (€€€)
A former station house lovingly transformed in keeping with the original 1860s stone building to provide a unique hotel and award-winning restaurant. Exquisite rooms have been created with individual style.
www.thestationhousehotel.com
✉ **Kilmessan** ☎ **046 902 5239; fax 046 902 5588**

Co Wicklow
Downshire House (€€)
Georgian-style family run hotel on Blessington's pretty tree-lined main street. The individually decorated rooms have old-fashioned charm. An ideal base for touring the Wicklow Mountains. Restaurant (▶ 99).
www.downshirehouse.com
✉ **Blessington** ☎ **045 865 199; fax 045 865 335**

Glendalough Hotel (€€)
Victorian building nestled amid amazing mountain scenery within the Wicklow Mountains National Park. Furnished throughout with traditional Irish fittings, most of the well-equipped bedrooms have views of the surrounding hills.
www.glendaloughhotel.com
✉ **Glendalough** ☎ **0404 45135; fax 0404 45141**

Hunters Hotel (€€)
Squeaky floors and the scent of old wood smoke add to the charm of this rambling coaching inn dating from 1700. The chintzy lounge is filled with fresh flowers. Lush gardens run down to the river.
www.hunters.ie ✉ **Newrath Bridge, Rathnew** ☎ **0404 40106; fax 0404 40338**

Sheepwalk House (€)
Hospitable Georgian guesthouse with many original features. The charming bedrooms are all different: the timbered room has a four-poster bed and two rooms have sea views through huge picture windows. Magnificent views of the coast.
www.sheepwalk.com
✉ **Avoca** ☎ **0402 35189; fax 0402 35789**

AA Hotel Booking Service
A free, fast and easy way to find a place to stay for your short break, holiday or business trip. Full listings of Irish hotels and B&Bs available through the service can be found and booked via the AA's website:
www.theAA.com

Department Stores & Malls

Street Markets

Today the streets of Dublin are not so blessed with lively, colourful street markets, and of the few that remain most are under cover; but there are some still worth a visit. Moore Street Market, off Henry Street, is the most authentic and is famous as the spiritual home of Molly Malone. Open daily, it is primarily a fruit and vegetable market but all sorts of bargains are now sold here.

Arnotts

Huge department store stocking everything you could possibly want, from clothes and cosmetics to home entertainment, furnishings and sports gear, all at reasonable prices.
✉ **12 Henry Street** ☎ **872 1111 or 805 0400** 🚇 **Connolly/Tara Street** 🚌 **Cross-city buses**

Avoca

Irish to the core, this department store stocks its own ranges of innovative items, combining traditional with fashionable, including clothing, accessories, gifts and household items. Don't miss the food hall and café.
✉ **11–13 Suffolk Street** ☎ **677 4215** 🚇 **Pearse** 🚌 **Cross-city buses**

Brown Thomas

Sophisticated store on Dublin's most fashionable shopping street showcasing designer clothes and other high-class goods such as cosmetics, household items and lots more. Quite pricey, but look out for the sales – you could find a bargain.
✉ **88–95 Grafton Street** ☎ **605 6666** 🚇 **Pearse** 🚌 **Cross-city buses**

Clery's

This Dublin institution has had a face-lift, giving it a trendier image. There is a huge range of goods, but it is ideal for Irish gifts. Known for its theatrical window displays and the gold-embossed clock outside.
✉ **18–27 O'Connell Street Lower** ☎ **878 6000** 🚇 **Tara Street/Connolly** 🚌 **Cross-city buses**

ILAC Centre

Dublin's oldest shopping mall has had a face-lift and now houses the sparkling new Roches department store on five floors. Other shops include bargain outlets and trendy clothes stores.
✉ **Henry Street** ☎ **704 1460** 🚇 **Connolly/Tara Street, Jervis LUAS** 🚌 **Cross-city buses**

Jervis Centre

You will find most British main-street chains – such as Argos and Debenhams – at this modern shopping complex on several floors. Huge top-floor food court.
✉ **Henry Street** ☎ **878 1323** 🚇 **Connolly/Tara Street, Jervis LUAS** 🚌 **Cross-city buses**

Marks and Spencer

This British store sells good-quality and affordable women's, men's and children's clothes, household items and lots more.
✉ **15–20 Grafton Street** ☎ **679 7855** 🚇 **Pearse** 🚌 **Cross-city buses**

Powerscourt Townhouse

Classy boutiques, high-quality handicraft and antique shops, art galleries and restaurants surround the inner courtyard of an elegant converted 18th-century Georgian town house.
✉ **59 William Street South** ☎ **679 4144** 🚇 **Tara Street/Pearse** 🚌 **Cross-city buses**

St Stephen's Green Centre

Bright and airy, this arcade in Victorian style is enclosed by a glass roof. The three floors house a mix of international chain stores and specialist shops. The top-floor café has fine views over the green.
✉ **St Stephen's Green/top of Grafton Street** ☎ **478 0888** 🚇 **Pearse** 🚌 **Cross-city buses**

Art & Antiques

Apollo Gallery
A collection of work by primarily Irish painters, plus some sculpture and prints. Famous patrons have included film stars Sylvester Stallone and Robert De Niro.
✉ 51c Dawson Street ☎ 671 2609 🚉 Pearse 🚌 Cross-city buses

Artselect
Watercolours and oil on canvas, graphics and photography, sculpture, kinetic art, ceramics and glasswork – the varied exhibits of new and established Irish talent are rotated on a regular basis.
✉ Meeting House Square, Temple Bar ☎ 635 1046 🚉 Tara Street 🚌 Cross-city buses

Graphics Studio Gallery
The oldest print gallery in Ireland, dealing with contemporary original prints, representing the works of over 100 of Ireland's most well-known or emerging artists.
✉ Through The Arch, off Cope Street, Temple Bar ☎ 679 8021 🚉 Tara Street 🚌 Cross-city buses

IB Jorgensen Fine Art
Expect to pay top prices at this exclusive gallery owned by Ireland's famous fashion designer. The fine art here includes works by the likes of Jack Yeats, Mary Swanzy and Walter Frederick Osborne.
✉ 29 Molesworth Street ☎ 661 9758 🚉 Pearse 🚌 Cross-city buses

John Farrington Antiques
The rich and famous visit this small shop filled with silver, glass, Irish furniture and the most sought-after items – antique jewellery.
✉ 32 Drury Street ☎ 679 1899 🚉 Pearse 🚌 Cross-city buses

Lemon Street Gallery
Work by a variety of international and Irish artists is showcased at this refreshing gallery, with a relaxed atmosphere. There is a constant turnover of exhibits.
✉ Lemon Street, off Grafton Street ☎ 671 0244 🚉 Pearse 🚌 Cross-city buses

O'Sullivan Antiques
You'll find all sorts here, from mahogany furniture and garden statues to gilt mirrors and delicate glass. Owner Chantal O'Sullivan is an expert on the Irish antiques scene.
✉ 43–44 Francis Street ☎ 454 1143 🚌 Cross-city buses

Silver Shop
The imaginative antique silver and silver-plate items sold here make an ideal special gift. Prices can be high, but there are also some more reasonably priced pieces.
✉ First Floor, Powerscourt Townhouse Centre, William Street South ☎ 679 4147 🚉 Pearse 🚌 Cross-city buses

Timepiece Antique Clocks
Intriguing shop where 18th- and 19th-century antique clocks are painstakingly restored and sold on the premises. The majority are Irish long-case clocks, but there are also some ornate French pieces.
✉ 57–58 Patrick Street ☎ 454 0774 🚌 Cross-city buses

Antique Quarter
Georgian Irish furniture and silver embodies some of the finest craftmanship of the late 18th and early 19th centuries. Francis Street, just around the corner from St Patrick's Cathedral, has become one of the focuses of Dublin's antique trade. Here you'll find a whole cluster of shops selling elegant, good-quality antiques and bric-à-brac.

Books & Music

Bodhrán

The simple frame drum or *bodhrán*, pronounced 'bough-rawn', has been played in Ireland for centuries, and gained worldwide fame in the 1960s with the rise of the Irish band The Chieftans. It is made out of beautifully decorated wood with animal skin (usually goat skin) stretched over the frame. It is played with a double-ended stick.

Cathach Books

An antiquarian bookshop stocking Irish-interest books with the emphasis on 20th-century literature.

✉ **10 Duke Street** ☎ **671 8676**
🚊 **Pearse** 🚌 **Cross-city buses**

Celtic Note

A great place for music lovers, this small, specialist Irish store sells music of all descriptions, from folk and traditional ballads to rock and contemporary.

✉ **12 Nassau Street** ☎ **670 4157** 🚊 **Pearse** 🚌 **Cross-city buses**

Charles Byrne

Charming instrument shop established in 1870, famous for its knowledge of stringed instruments. The shop has a large range of hand-made *bodhráns* (drums).

✉ **21–22 Stephen Street Lower** ☎ **478 1773** 🚊 **Pearse** 🚌 **Cross-city buses**

Claddagh Records

Traditional and folk music emporium selling just about every recording that is currently available. And what you can't find the knowledgeable staff will track down for you.

✉ **2 Cecilia Street, Temple Bar** ☎ **677 0262** 🚊 **Tara Street** 🚌 **Cross-city buses**

Dublin Writers Museum Bookshop

In a city famous for its literary connections, it is appropriate that this excellent bookshop is inside the Dublin Writers Museum.

✉ **18–19 Parnell Street North** ☎ **872 2077** 🚌 **Cross-city buses**

Eason's

This vast general bookstore, with several branches all over the city, carries a huge variety of books and the widest-range of magazines, plus stationery, art supplies and music. Also has a café.

✉ **40 O'Connell Street** ☎ **873 3811** 🚊 **Tara Street/Connolly** 🚌 **Cross-city buses**

Hodges Figgis

Well-known bookstore established in 1768, spread across three floors. It's a maze of books covering all subjects, with an emphasis on Celtic and Irish history, culture and literature.

✉ **56–58 Dawson Street** ☎ **677 4754** 🚊 **Pearse** 🚌 **Cross-city buses**

McCullough Pigott's

Irish music enthusiasts can spend hours thumbing through the sheet music and gazing at the musical instruments on display in this highly respected music shop.

✉ **25 Suffolk Street** ☎ **677 3138** 🚊 **Pearse** 🚌 **Cross-city buses**

Waltons

Irish musical instrument specialist with an amazing display of harps, *bodhráns*, whistles, pipes, flutes, banjos, mandolins, bouzoukis and accordions.

✉ **69–70 South Great George's Street** ☎ **475 0661** 🚊 **Pearse** 🚌 **Cross-city buses**

Winding Stair

Lovely dusty old bookshop that encourages you to browse the bookshelves crammed full of mostly second-hand books. You can also take coffee in the café, overlooking the river.

✉ **40 Ormond Quay Lower** ☎ **873 3292** 🚊 **Tara Street** 🚌 **Cross-city buses**

Food & Drink

Avoca Food Hall
Packed with enticing produce such as oils, preserves, pastas and biscuits, all under the Avoca label, this splendid food hall has to be seen to be believed.

✉ **11–13 Suffolk Street** ☎ **677 4215** 🚇 **Pearse** 🚌 **Cross-city buses**

Bewleys Oriental Café
Bewley's teashops sell their own exclusive teas and coffees in attractive containers. They also offer a range of cakes, biscuits and chocolates. Also a branch at Westmorland Street.

✉ **78–79 Grafton Street** ☎ **635 5470** 🚇 **Pearse** 🚌 **Cross-city buses**

Butlers Chocolates
Mrs Bailey-Butler's secret recipe for luxurious hand-made chocolates has been handed down through the generations since 1932. You can buy them pre-boxed or make your own choice from the loose counter and have them gift-wrapped.

✉ **51A Grafton Street** ☎ **616 7004** 🚇 **Pearse** 🚌 **Cross-city buses**

Celtic Whiskey Shop
Apart from having one of the best selections of Irish whiskies in the city, there are tempting hand-made Irish chocolates and an assortment of wines and liqueurs for sale. Daily tastings.

✉ **27–28 Dawson Street** ☎ **675 9744** 🚇 **Pearse** 🚌 **Cross-city buses**

Gallic Kitchen
The smell draws you to this pâtisserie, selling freshly made potato cakes, quiches, pies and cakes, plus other tasty treats to take away. You can also buy their goods from the Temple Bar Food Market on Saturdays.

✉ **49 Francis Street** ☎ **454 4912** 🚌 **Cross-city buses**

Le Maison des Gourmets
The amazing display in the window offers a taster of the treats within – the finest olives, tasty savouries, oils, breads and patés, all finely packaged to take away.

✉ **15 Castle Market** ☎ **672 7258** 🚇 **Pearse** 🚌 **Cross-city buses**

Magills
Old-fashioned delicatessen piled high with charcuterie, Irish cheeses and patés, smoked salmon, exotic chutneys, herbs and spices, and every kind of delicacy you can think of. Loved by generations of Dubliners.

✉ **14 Clarendon Street** ☎ **671 3830** 🚇 **Pearse Street** 🚌 **Cross-city buses**

Mitchell & Son Wine Merchants
The oldest and possibly finest wine merchant in Dublin stocks unusual and exclusive vintages in the basement, along with all the usual brands.

✉ **21 Kildare Street** ☎ **676 0766** 🚇 **Pearse** 🚌 **Cross-city buses**

Old Jameson Distilley
The shop at the distillery sells a range of Irish whiskey-flavoured items – cakes, truffles, jams, fudge, chutney and marmalade – but don't forget a bottle of the real thing.

✉ **Bow Street** ☎ **807 2355** 🚇 **Smithfield LUAS** 🚌 **83**

Meeting House Square Food Market
Every Saturday – except over Christmas – local traders turn out between 9:30 and 5 to sell their fare at this food-lovers haven. Amazing smells waft from the stalls displaying a variety of produce ranging from Japanese sushi to Mexican burritos. Local Irish foods include cheeses, fresh oysters, home-made breads and quiches, cakes, jams and yogurts, and those with a sweet tooth will enjoy the chocolates or freshly made waffles. The only drawback is you probably won't get home without eating your purchases along the way.

Fashion

Second-hand Bargains

Dublin has several vintage and second-hand clothing stores where you might discover a genuine treasure. Some items may have been loaned out to wardrobe film sets, so you could even find a celebrity cast-off. Eager Beaver (✉ 17 Crown Alley ☎ 677 3342) in Temple Bar specialises in next-to-new clothing and Flip (✉ 3–4 Upper Fownes Street ☎ 671 4299), also in Temple Bar, is the place for trendy shoppers on the trail of second-hand jeans, baseball jackets and other items of Americana. Jenny Vander (✉ 50 Drury Street ☎ 677 0406) sells luxury evening wear for that special occasion.

Alias Tom

Everything you need to dress a man from head to foot by top international names such as Armani and Dublin-born designers like John Rocha. The staff are attentive without being intrusive.
✉ **Duke House, Duke Lane**
☎ **671 5443** 🚇 **Pearse**
🚌 **Cross-city buses**

A Wear

This Irish main-street chain sells fashionable clothes and accessories at low prices, allowing you to follow the dictates of fashion without breaking the bank.
✉ **26 Grafton Street** ☎ **671 7200** 🚇 **Pearse** 🚌 **Cross-city buses**

BT2

An offshoot of Brown Thomas (▶ 104) targeting a more youthful shopper looking for trendy casual clothes by the likes of DKNY, French Connection and Calvin Klein.
✉ **28 Grafton Street** ☎ **605 6666, ext 1200** 🚇 **Pearse** 🚌 **Cross-city buses**

Costume

Costume's diverse range of elegant clothes highlights some of Europe's most innovative designers – Anna Sui, Alice Temperley and local designer Leigh Tucker.
✉ **10–11 Castle Market** ☎ **679 4188** 🚇 **Pearse** 🚌 **Cross-city buses**

Louis Copeland

Every well-dressed Irish man or society figure aims to own a Louis Copeland, the ultimate in made-to-measure suits. Even one off the peg made by a top designer will do very nicely. There are

other branches throughout the city.
✉ **30 Pembroke Street Lower**
☎ **661 0110** 🚌 **10A**

Louise Kennedy

Hailed as Ireland's leading designer, Kennedy's tasteful clothing is sold alongside a crystal collection and luxury accessories, in a restored Georgian house that exudes style, just like her clothing.
✉ **56 Merrion Square** ☎ **662 0056** 🚇 **Pearse** 🚌 **Cross-city buses**

Smock

This tiny boutique creates a cosy atmosphere where you can try on the simple but slightly quirky women's clothing by mostly Irish names such as Ali Malek, AF Vandevorft and Easton Pearson.
✉ **20–22 Essex Street West, Temple Bar** ☎ **613 9000** 🚇 **Tara Street** 🚌 **Cross-city buses**

Susan Hunter

Expensive but irresistible little shop selling exquisite silk lingerie made by all the big names such as La Perla, Aubade and Tuttabankem. Frequently visited by the glitterati.
✉ **13 Westbury Mall** ☎ **679 1271** 🚇 **Pearse** 🚌 **Cross-city buses**

Thomas Pink

Founded in 1984 by the Mullen brothers, this is the place to come for the ideal complement to your Louis Copeland suit. Perfectly cut shirts in every conceivable design, style and cloth, plus silk ties, cuff links and more.
✉ **29 Dawson Street** ☎ **670 3647** 🚇 **Pearse** 🚌 **Cross-city buses**

Irish Crafts & Design

Blarney Woollen Mills
An array of traditional hand-woven products – sweaters, rugs, hats – from the Cork-based mills, plus top-notch Irish tweeds, lace and linen, alongside names like Belleek and Waterford Crystal.
✉ 21–23 Nassau Street ☎ 671 0068 🚇 Pearse 🚌 Cross-city buses

Cleo
This small shop, run by three generations of the Joyce family since 1936, sells authentic hand-knits and clothes made from traditional Irish natural fibres. Items are expensive but unique.
✉ 18 Kildare Street ☎ 676 1421 🚇 Pearse 🚌 Cross-city buses

DESIGNYard
This Victorian warehouse has been converted into a stunning gallery showcasing original contemporary designs by Irish potters, jewellers and craftspeople.
✉ 12 East Essex Street ☎ 677 8453 🚇 Tara Street 🚌 Cross-city buses

House of Ireland
Quality craft shop geared towards tourists, stacked high with mainly woollen and tweed clothes made in Ireland. You can also buy cut crystal, fine china and other items that make ideal gifts. .
✉ 38 Nassau Street ☎ 671 4543 🚇 Pearse 🚌 Cross-city buses

Kevin and Howlin
A family-run shop considered the best place to buy Donegal tweed clothing. These hardwearing items from jackets and waistcoats to hats and ties, come in many patterns and colours and are available in modern and traditional styles.
✉ 31 Nassau Street ☎ 677 0257 🚇 Pearse 🚌 Cross-city buses

Kilkenny Centre
For stylish items made in Ireland, look no further. The amazing selection of pottery, glassware, jewellery and fashion is mainly traditional, with a touch of creativity.
✉ 6 Nassau Street ☎ 677 7066 🚇 Pearse 🚌 Cross-city buses

Louis Mulcahy
This elegant store sells the work of one of Ireland's most prolific potters. Here you can buy hand-thrown pots, urns, vases, teapots and other ceramics, plus a selection of beautiful hand-woven wall hangings.
✉ 46 Dawson Street ☎ 670 9311 🚇 Pearse 🚌 Cross-city buses

Trinity Craft Centre
Housed in a 19th-century warehouse near the canals, this design centre has around 35 studios for inspired potters, jewellers and textile designers who work and sell their hand-crafted wares here.
✉ 677 Pearse Street ☎ 677 5655 🚇 Grand Canal Dock 🚌 2, 3

Whichcraft
A wonderful shop featuring the work of some Ireland's best craft workers and artists. They reach new heights of innovation with their modern interpretations using glass, metal, ceramic and wood.
✉ Cow's Lane, Temple Bar ☎ 474 1011 🚇 Tara Street 🚌 Cross-city buses

Traditional Versus Modern
A growing number of shops in Dublin displayf home interior goods produced by Irish craftspeople and local designers turning their skills to furniture and other items. Irish fashion designer John Rocha has brought Waterford Crystal up to date with his clean, minimalist designs. Beautiful objects in stone, wood, glass and other natural materials can be bought in both contemporary and traditional designs. Jewellery has a special place in Dublin's heart, which lives on in the exquisite replicas of the Tara Brooch, Claddagh rings and Celtic knots, mixing modern design with tradition.

Where to take the Children

Just for Kids

There should be no problem satisfying hungry children in Dublin, which has more than enough fast-food outlets. Check out TGI Friday's (🖂 St Stephen's Green ☎ 478 1233), who understand what kids want; or Captain Americas (44 Grafton Street ☎ 671 5266), with a rock 'n roll theme and affordable American-style food; on Sunday, clowns entertain the young ones. At Thunder Road Café (Fleet Street, Temple Bar ☎ 679 4057) they can enjoy the huge video screens and the Harley Davidson in the window, while Milano (🖂 Dawson Street ☎ 670 7744) is Ireland's equivalent to Pizza Hut.

The Ark

This purpose-built cultural centre aimed at 4- to 14-year-olds offers stimulating performances for children in the indoor theatre, outdoor amphitheatre (summer only) and workshop space.

🖂 11a Eustace Street, Temple Bar ☎ 670 7788; www.ark.ie ⏰ Mon–Fri 9:30–4; call for activity times 🚇 Tara Street 🚌 Cross-city buses 🅿 Good

Bram Stoker Dracula Experience

Not for the very young or faint-hearted, but most children's imaginations will run wild during this spine-chilling experience that uses the very latest technology to startling effect (➤ 34).

The Chimney

A glass-walled escalator transports you to the top of the old distillery chimney where, from the enclosed glass observation deck, there are panoramic views over the city. In the great Dublin tradition of naming statues and edifices, the Chimney is now affectionately known as 'the flue with the view'. In December children come here to visit Santa Claus – the base is turned into a Christmas grotto.

🖂 Smithfield Village ☎ 817 3800 ⏰ Mon–Sat, daily 10–5:30 (may be subject to seasonal change) 🚇 Smithfield LUAS 🚌 83 🅿 Moderate 🅿 Good

Clara Lara Fun Park

A 40ha (100-acre) adventure park set in woodland and lakes in the heart of the Wicklow Mountains. Fun rides, mostly involving water, include Aqua Shuttle – the highest slide in Ireland – rafts and boats. For those who prefer to stay on dry land there are go-karts, woodland play areas and assault courses. Also picnic areas and a restaurant.

🖂 Vale of Clara, Rathdrum, Co Wicklow ☎ 0404 46161 ⏰ May–Sep, daily 10:30–6 🅿 Expensive 🅿 Few

Dublin Zoo

An ideal family day out. Over 700 animals from around the world roam this modern zoo dedicated to conservation and education. Children will love Monkey Island and the Pet Care Area, and be sure to check out the newborn babies and feeding programmes (➤ 43).

Dvblinia

An entertaining audio-visual journey through medieval Dublin, where life-sized wax models and genuine objects discovered locally are used in authentic reconstructions (➤ 44).

Fry Model Railway

A 240sq m (2,580 sq ft) railway layout that displays the unique collection of hand-made models of Irish trains, from the beginning of rail travel to the present day. In the grounds of Malahide Castle (➤ 57), 13km (8 miles) outside Dublin.

🖂 Malahide Castle, Malahide ☎ 846 3779 ⏰ Apr–Sep, Mon–Thu & Sat 10–1, 2–5, Sun & public hols 2–6 🚇 Malahide (then 10-minute walk) 🚌 42 🅿 Moderate 🅿 Good

Guinness Storehouse

Guinness may be strictly for adults, but that should not deter children from enjoying the interactive exhibits at

this fascinating museum inside Ireland's famous brewery. Sound effects and old machinery trundling away in the background add to the atmosphere. One thing the kids won't be able to do is collect their sample of the black stuff in the bar on the top floor – they'll have to make do with the fantastic views over Dublin (► 19).

Lambert Puppet Theatre

This purpose-built puppet theatre has been delighting children with imaginative and enjoyable re-enactments of famous fairy-tales for generations.

⊠ **5 Clifton Lane, Monkstown** ☎ **280 0974** ◎ **Performances Sat, Sun 3:30; or by arrangement for groups** 🚇 **Monkstown/ Salthill** 🚌 **7, 7A** 💷 **Expensive** ♿ **Good (no access to upper level)**

National Sea Life Centre

On the seafront at Bray, the centre's main attraction is the 'Lair of the Octopus', a re-creation of the undersea world inhabited by these strange beasts. Other creatures you can have a close encounter with include seahorses, sharks and giant Japanese spider crabs. On-site restaurant and gift shop.

www.sealife.ie

⊠ **Strand Road, Bray** ☎ **286 6939** ◎ **Daily from 10am; call for display times and winter openings** 🚇 **Bray (5-minute walk)** 🚌 **45, 84** 💷 **Expensive** ♿ **Good**

National Wax Museum

With more than 300 exhibits to see – from rock stars and sports heroes to the cult cartoon family the Simpsons – this museum will certainly entertain the kids on a wet afternoon. Most youngsters enjoy the hall of mirrors, while the older kids indulge in the chamber of horrors (► 60).

Newgrange Farm

Kids will love this hands-on farm, to the west of Newgrange tomb, where they can feed the animals and view the exotic birds in the aviary. The farmer demonstrates how to shoe a horse and you can see the sheepdogs at work. Every Sunday the 'sheep derby' takes place: a highly amusing race where teddies are used as jockeys and each child is allocated a sheep to support. Best visited by car as public transport is limited.

⊠ **Newgrange, off N51 between Drogheda and Slane** ☎ **041 982 4119** ◎ **Easter–end Aug, daily 10–6** 💷 **Moderate** ♿ **Good**

Viking Splash Tours

Fun and educational, this exciting tour takes you through Viking Dublin aboard a reconditioned World War II amphibious bus before ploughing into the Grand Canal to conclude the trip on water. Departs from Bull Alley and Stephen's Green North.

www.vikingsplashtours.com

⊠ **64–65 Patrick Street** ☎ **707 6000** ◎ **Mid-Feb–May, Nov Tue–Sun; Jun–Oct daily. Tour times: every 30 minutes 10am–noon, 1:30–5 (Sun first tour 10:30, Nov last tour 3:30)** 💷 **Expensive** ♿ **None**

All Aboard

Dublin Bus (☎ 873 4222) operate a city tour aboard an open-top bus. There are 19 stops at the more popular attractions where you can hop on and off as often as you wish – guaranteed to stop the kids getting restless. If you choose to stay on board, the tour – with a live commentary – takes 1 hour 15 minutes. Tours begin in O'Connell Street and run every 10 minutes from 9:30 to 3 and every 15 minutes from 3 to 5.

Theatres & Cinemas

Out of Town
Apart from the many theatres and cinemas to choose from in the city centre, there are other good options in the surrounding suburbs. A 20-minute drive northwest of the city at Blanchardstown Shopping Centre is a UCI multiplex (☎ 812 8383) showing all the latest blockbusters, as well as the Draíocht Theatre (☎ 885 2622), an arts centre with two theatres presenting classic plays and brand new works. The Liffey Valley Centre in Clondalkin, 20 minutes southwest, has a Ster Century cinema (☎ 605 5700), Ireland's biggest multiplex, with 24 screens, including The Big Fell, Europe's largest.

Theatres
Abbey Theatre
The Abbey was built for the National Theatre of Ireland in 1966 and the performances here are first class; many first runs go on to Broadway or the West End. In the basement The Peacock Theatre is a platform for up-and-coming writers.
✉ 26 Abbey Street Lower ☎ 878 7222 🚇 Connolly/ Tara Street 🚌 Cross-city buses

Focus Theatre
Movie star Gabriel Byrne regularly appeared at this venue, established in 1967. It has a reputation for putting on challenging plays from new and established writers; modern and classic drama.
✉ 6 Pembroke Place, off Pembroke Street ☎ 676 3071 🚌 10A, 15X, 25X, 49X

Gaiety Theatre
This traditional theatre, with velvet curtains and boxes, hosts a diverse schedule of drama, music and opera; also popular for pantomimes.
✉ King Street South ☎ 677 1717 🚇 Tara 🚌 Cross-city buses

Gate Theatre
A beautiful Georgian building where inspired new works are staged in the elegant auditorium, as well as established classics (▶ 47).
✉ 1 Cavendish Row, Parnell Square ☎ 874 4045 🚇 Connolly 🚌 Cross-city buses

Olympia Theatre
Luminaries who have taken the stage at this old-style variety hall, opened in 1749, range from Noel Coward to comedian Jack Dee. It now mounts mostly mainstream shows including musicals, stand-up comedy, pantos, and has played host to major rock and pop acts.
✉ 72 Dame Street ☎ 679 3323 🚇 Tara Street 🚌 Cross-city buses

Project Arts Centre
This former print works is now a centre for young theatre groups staging experimental performances.
✉ 39 Essex Street East ☎ 679 6622 🚇 Tara Street 🚌 Cross-city buses

Cinemas
Irish Film Institute
Open to members and guests, this modern centre has two screens showing excellent arthouse cinema and is home to the Irish Film Archive. Film buffs will want to browse in the bookshop. Restaurant and bar.
✉ 6 Eustace Street ☎ 679 5744 🚇 Tara Street 🚌 Cross-city buses

Savoy
An old-fashioned movie theatre with modern concessions: five wide screens, one the largest in Dublin, and Dolby sound systems. The cinema hosts premieres of Irish films and all the latest blockbusters.
✉ O'Connell Street ☎ 874 6000 🚌 Cross-city buses

UGC Multiplex
This huge centre houses a cinema with 17 screens (showing current releases), simulated rides, computer games, themed bars and restaurants.
✉ Parnell Centre, Parnell Street ☎ 872 8444 🚇 Connolly 🚌 Cross-city buses

Live Music & Clubs

Live Music

Ambassador Theatre
This impressive late-Victorian building at the top of O'Connell Street, which has taken on many guises over the years, is now a small rock and pop concert venue.
✉ Parnell Street ☎ 0818 719300 🚉 Tara Street/Connolly 🚌 Cross-city buses

Bank of Ireland Arts Centre
Classical recitals of modern and standard music by amateur and professional groups are held at this small venue with only 200 seats.
✉ 2 Foster Place, College Green ☎ 671 2261 🚉 Tara Street 🚌 Cross-city buses

The Helix
Opened in 2002 on the university campus, the Helix has proved to be a worthy addition to Dublin's live music scene. The stunning state-of-the-art complex has three performance venues and an impressive schedule of classical music, drama and mainstream rock and pop.
✉ Dublin City University, Collins Avenue, Glasnevin ☎ 700 7000 🚌 13A, 16, 16A, 103

National Concert Hall
This fine Georgian building is Dublin's biggest and most prestigious classical music venue and home of the RTÉ National Symphony Orchestra. The modern auditorium, with superb acoustics, hosts a full calendar of events.
✉ Earlsfort Terrace ☎ 417 0000 🚉 Pearse 🚌 Cross-city buses

The Point
A vast auditorium housed in a former tram depot with a capacity of between 4,000 and 6,000; the premier venue for all visiting music and dance superstars. The impressive role call ranges from the Rolling Stones and Coldplay to the Bolshoi Ballet and Riverdance.
✉ East Link Bridge, North Wall Quay ☎ 836 6777 🚌 53A

Temple Bar Music Centre
A premier music venue staging music, dance, theatre and art performed by a high calibre of home-grown and international talent.
✉ Curved Street ☎ 670 9202 🚉 Tara Street 🚌 Cross-city buses

Clubs

Lillie's Bordello
You need to dress to impress to enter this trendy nightspot, where it's cooler to spot the celebrity among the beautiful people than boogie to the house, chart and oldie music.
✉ Adam Court, Grafton Street ☎ 679 9204 🚉 Pearse 🚌 Cross-city buses

POD
Housed in the stone vaults of an old railway station, 'Place of Dance' is a stylish, futuristic space. The hottest DJs spin a mix of happy house and dance floor favourites for the crowd.
✉ Harcourt Street ☎ 478 0225 🚌 Cross-city buses

Rí Rá
A diverse crowd immerse themselves in the sounds of a variety of music at this relaxed and fashionable club.
✉ Dame Court ☎ 677 4835 🚉 Tara Street 🚌 Cross-city buses

Dance the Night Away
Nightlife culture in Dublin is thriving and there are many good dance clubs well worth a visit. Apart from the old favourites, places tend to come and go, so it's more a case of looking to see what's on that night rather than at the venue itself. Most good dance nights are organized by promoters and staged in different places around the city. *The Event Guide,* distributed free in bars and cafés throughout the city, has comprehensive night-by-night listings of who and what's on, when and where.

Pubs & Bars

Which Pub?

There are so many pubs in Dublin it's almost impossible to choose where to go; here are a few more to help you decide.

Dawson Lounge

A tiny doorway and a narrow flight of steps lead to the smallest pub in Dublin – worth having a look even if you don't stay for a pint.

✉ 25 Dawson Street ☎ 671 0311 🚆 Pearse 🚌 Cross-city buses

McDaids

A small, dark high-ceilinged bar, well known for its literary connections.

✉ 3 Harry Street ☎ 679 4395 🚆 Pearse 🚌 Cross-city buses

Messrs Maguire

Beer is brewed in the basement of this popular haunt, with lots of nooks and crannies.

✉ 1–2 Burgh Quay ☎ 670 5777 🚆 Tara Street 🚌 Cross-city buses

O'Shea's Merchant

Nobody can resist joining in with the traditional music and dance that takes place every night.

✉ 12 Lower Bridge Street ☎ 679 6793 🚌 51B, 78A

The Bank

This building has been splendidly adapted to preserve its Victorian grandeur – stained-glass ceilings, hand-carved plasterwork and mosaic flooring – just as it was when the Belfast Bank first opened here in 1895.

✉ 20–22 College Green ☎ 677 0677 H🚆 Tara Street 🚌 Cross-city buses

Brazen Head

The Brazen Head claims to be the oldest bar in Dublin; memorabilia of the pub's history is displayed on the walls. It serves one of the best pints of Guinness in Dublin, along with good food and lots of old-world charm.

✉ 20 Bridge Street Lower ☎ 679 5186 🚌 51B, 78A

Café en Seine

A trendy young crowd comes to this spectacular place to drink in extravagant style. Over-the-top fittings include a fabulous wood and marble bar and real trees 12m (40ft) high.

✉ 40 Dawson Street ☎ 677 4369 🚆 Pearse 🚌 Cross-city buses

Doheny & Nesbitt

A glorious old pub over three floors with a great selection of whiskeys and stouts, and lively *craic*. Popular with politicians and journalists.

✉ 5 Baggot Street Lower ☎ 676 2945 🚌 10A, 15X, 25X, 49X

Hogan's

Huge, fashionable hang-out packed with Dublin's bright young things getting in the swing with a few drinks and background music before moving on to the nearby dance clubs.

✉ 35 South Great George's Street ☎ 677 5904 🚌 Cross-city buses

John Kehoe

If nooks and crannies are your scene, this atmospheric pub is just the place. The mahogany interior has a wonderful Victorian bar where excellent beer is sold.

✉ 9 Anne Street South ☎ 677 8312 🚆 Pearse 🚌 Cross-city buses

Long Hall

Time seems to have stood still at this traditional Irish pub. The grand Victorian interior has retained ornate wood carvings, chandeliers and a beautiful pendulum clock over 200 years old.

✉ 51 South Great George's Street ☎ 475 1590 🚆 Tara Street 🚌 Cross-city buses

Mulligans

A Guinness drinkers' institution since 1820, legendary for its perfectly poured pint of Guinness, and also for the fact that John F Kennedy drank here, as a journalist in 1947.

✉ 8 Poolbeg Street ☎ 677 5582 🚆 Tara Street 🚌 Cross-city buses

Stag's Head

James Joyce drank at this characterful pub, built in 1770. Carved wood, stained glass, shiny brass and ironwork give a church-like atmosphere, although the stuffed stags' heads on the walls don't conform. Good pub grub.

✉ 1 Dame Court ☎ 679 3701 🚆 Tara Street 🚌 Cross-city buses

Sport

Gaelic Games

Gaelic football and hurling are played all over County Dublin and the All-Ireland finals take place before sell-out crowds in early and late September. These fast and furious games are promoted by the Gaelic Athletic Association – Ireland's largest sporting and cultural organization – based at Croke Park, where there is a museum (▶ 45) devoted to Ireland's national games.

Croke Park Stadium, St Joseph's Avenue ☎ 836 3222 🚌 3, 11, 11A, 16, 16A

Golf

Golf is the fastest growing sport in the area, with over 60 courses to choose from. The most famous are Ireland's oldest golf club, Royal Dublin, and Portmarnock, created by Bernhard Langer. The majority of clubs will accept visitors. A complete list of private courses can be obtained from the Golfing Union of Ireland (www.gui.ie; 269 4111)

Portmarock ✉ Portmarnock, Co Dublin ☎ 846 0611
Royal Dublin ✉ Bull Island, Dollymount ☎ 833 6346

Horse Racing

The flat season runs from March to November and the National Hunt from October to April. There are several courses around Dublin, but the most prestigious are Leopardstown, which has both flat and jumps, and hosts the Hennessy Gold Cup in February, and the Curragh, home of Irish flat racing and a principal venue since 1741.

Leopardstown Racecourse
✉ **Leopardstown Road, Foxrock** ☎ 289 3607 🚌 86, 118
The Curragh ✉ Co Kildare ☎ 045 441 205 🚌 **Bus Éireann 126 (extra buses on race days)** 🚆 **Kildare to Newbridge**

Rugby Union

Irish fans are very enthusiastic about their rugby. Details of fixtures for local clubs are listed in the newspapers, or you can soak up the atmosphere of a major international game at the national stadium, Lansdowne Road.

✉ **Lansdowne Road Stadium, Ballsbridge** ☎ 668 4601
🚆 **Lansdowne Road** 🚌 5, 7A, 45

Soccer

Over recent years a new generation of Irish soccer fans has emerged; though they are more fans of British teams, as most Irish internationals play for clubs such as Manchester United. But when international games take place Lansdowne Road is full to the brim. Shelbourne Rovers are one of Ireland's most successful clubs and their home ground is Tolka Park.

✉ **Tolka Park Stadium, Richmond Road** ☎ 837 5536
🚆 **Drumcondra** 🚌 3, 11, 11A, 13A, 16A, 33

Watersports

As Dublin is a coastal city watersports are a popular activity – windsurfing, waterskiing, scuba-diving and canoeing. Surfdock offers courses on all water-based sports for all levels; it also has a wind simulator and equipment for rent.

✉ **Grand Canal Dockyard, South Dock Road, Ringsend** ☎ 668 39 45 🚆 **Grand Canal Dock** 🚌 2, 3

On Your Bike

Dublin is perfect for cycling – all the main routes into the city have cycle lanes – though you will need a good lock to keep your bicycle safe. If you want to escape the crowded streets, Phoenix Park, not too far from the centre, is ideal for two wheels, or if you're feeling a little more ambitious you could cycle out to the coast at Howth or Dalkey. The more energetic cyclist may want to venture further into the Wicklow Mountains. Irish Cycling Safaris (www.cyclingsafaris.com; ☎ 260 0749), at the Belfield Bike Shop, University College Dublin, organize cycling tours.

What's On When

Listings

There are a number of publications useful for finding out what's on in the city. *The Irish Times* (Thursday edition) has a pullout section called *The Ticket* giving listings of forthcoming events and the *Evening Herald's* Thursday edition provides good coverage of what's on. Pick up a copy of the fortnightly publication *In Dublin* that lists most events, and look for *The Event Guide*, free from clubs, cafés and restaurants around the city, with comprehensive weekly listings.

January
New Year's Day Parade
Marching bands from all over the world come together in Dublin for the parade.

February
International Film Festival
The best Irish and international cinema is shown over a period of two weeks at this increasingly popular festival.

March
St Patrick's Day A popular date in Dublin's calendar, celebrated by a week of street entertainment, concerts, exhibitions and fireworks, building up to a huge parade on the day itself (17 March), usually starting near St Patrick's Cathedral.

May
Heineken Green Energy Music Festival Staged over the May bank holiday weekend, this major festival has featured top international stars since it began in the mid-1990s. There is normally an open-air concert in the grounds of Dublin Castle.

June
Bloomsday On 16 June each year, the day James Joyce set his novel *Ulysses*, Joycean fans celebrate the man and his works with tours, readings and seminars.

July
Dublin Jazz Festival A live, five-day schedule of music performed by artists from around the world. In Temple Bar and other locations.

Dublin Pride The gay and lesbian scene is flourishing in Dublin, and this month-long festival is celebrated in a big way. It includes a free open-air show at the Civic Offices.

August
Kerrygold Horse Show The best show horses and show jumpers descend on the RDS grounds in the first week of August for Ireland's equine highlight of the year.

Liffey Swim This has been a Dublin institution since 1924 – 400 or so people dive into the River Liffey in the centre of Dublin for a race through 2km (1.2 miles) of murky waters, while spectators line the bridges to watch.

September
Dublin Theatre Festival A two-week festival, among the most vibrant in Europe, attracting all the leading names from Dublin's drama scene. The many venues include the Abbey and the Gate theatres.

October
Dublin City Marathon On the last Monday in October thousands of enthusiastic runners turn out for the 42km (26-mile) run through the streets of Dublin.

Samhain An evening parade and fireworks for Dublin's Hallowe'en festival, based on the pagan festival of Samhain in celebration of the dead and the end of the Celtic summer.

December
Christmas National Hunt Festival A major four-day race meeting at Leopardstown racecourse.

Practical Matters

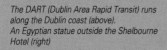

The DART (Dublin Area Rapid Transit) runs along the Dublin coast (above).
An Egyptian statue outside the Shelbourne Hotel (right)

TIME DIFFERENCES

GMT 12 noon	Ireland 12 noon	Germany 1PM →	USA (NY) 7AM ←	Netherlands 1PM →	Spain 1PM →

BEFORE YOU GO

WHAT YOU NEED

● Required ○ Suggested ▲ Not required	Some countries require a passport to remain valid for a minimum period (usually at least six months) beyond the date of entry – contact their consulate or embassy or your travel agent for details.	UK	Germany	USA	Netherlands	Spain
Passport/National Identity Card		●	●	●	●	●
Visa (regulations can change – check before booking your journey)		▲	▲	▲	▲	▲
Onward or Return Ticket		○	○	○	○	○
Health Inoculations		▲	▲	▲	▲	▲
Health Documentation (► 123, Health)		●	●	●	●	●
Travel Insurance		○	○	○	○	○
Driving Licence (national with English translation, or International)		●	●	●	●	●
Car Insurance Certificate		●	●	●	●	●
Car Registration Document		●	●	●	●	●

WHEN TO GO

Dublin

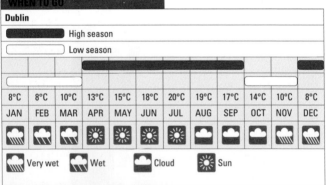

| | | | | High season | | | | | | | |
| | | | | Low season | | | | | | | |

8°C	8°C	10°C	13°C	15°C	18°C	20°C	19°C	17°C	14°C	10°C	8°C
JAN	FEB	MAR	APR	MAY	JUN	JUL	AUG	SEP	OCT	NOV	DEC

Very wet   Wet   Cloud   Sun

TOURIST OFFICES

In the UK
Tourism Ireland
103 Wigmore Street
London, W1U 1QF
☎ 0800 039 7000
Fax: 020 7493 9065

In the USA
Irish Tourist Board
345 Park Avenue
New York, NY 10154
☎ 212/418 0800
Fax: 212/371 9052

In Australia
Irish Tourist Board
5th Level
36 Carrington Street
Sydney, NSW 2000
☎ 02 9299 6177

POLICE 999	
FIRE 999	
AMBULANCE 999	
COASTAL RESCUE 999	

WHEN YOU ARE THERE

ARRIVING

Regular flights operate from Britain, mainland Europe and North America. The national airline is Aer Lingus (www.aerlingus.ie; ☎ 886 8844). Ryanair (www.ryanair.com; ☎ 812 1230) offers low-cost flights. Ferries from the UK sail to Dublin and Dun Laoghaire.

Dublin Airport
Kilometres to city centre

11 kilometres

🚇	N/A
🚌	30 minutes
🚗	20 minutes

Dun Laoghaire
Kilometres to city centre

12 kilometres

🚇	DART 20 minutes
🚌	30 minutes
🚗	20 minutes

MONEY

The euro is the official currency of the Republic of Ireland, which is divided into 100 cents. Coins come in denominations of 1, 2, 5, 10, 20 and 50 cents, €1 and €2, and notes come in €5, €10, €20, €50, €100, €200 and €500 denominations (the last two are rarely seen). The notes and one side of the coins are the same throughout the European single currency zone, but each country has a different design on one face of each of the coins.

TIME

Ireland observes Greenwich Mean Time (GMT), but from late March, when clocks are put forward one hour, until late October, summertime (GMT +1) operates.

CUSTOMS

YES
From another EU country for personal use (guidelines)
800 cigarettes, 200 cigars,
1 kilogram of tobacco
10 litres of spirits (over 22%)
20 litres of aperitifs
90 litres of wine, of which 60 litres can be sparkling wine
110 litres of beer

From a non-EU country for your personal use, the allowances are:
200 cigarettes OR
50 cigars OR 250 grams of tobacco
1 litre of spirits (over 22%)
2 litres of intermediary products (eg sherry) and sparkling wine
2 litres of still wine
50 grams of perfume
0.25 litres of eau de toilette
The value limit for goods is 175 euros

Travellers under 17 years of age are not entitled to the tobacco and alcohol allowances.

NO
Drugs, firearms, ammunition, offensive weapons, obscene material, unlicensed animals.

UK
205 3700

Germany
269 3011

USA
668 7122

Netherlands
269 3444

Spain
269 1640

WHEN YOU ARE THERE

TOURIST OFFICES

Irish Tourist Board
Baggot Street Bridge
Baggot Street
Dublin 2
www.ireland.travel.ie;
☎ 602 4000

Dublin Tourism Centre
St Andrew's Church
Suffolk Street
Dublin 2
www.visitdublin.com;
☎ 605 7700

Walk-in centres:
14 Upper O'Connell Street
Dublin Airport
Dun Laoghaire ferry terminal
The Square, Tallaght
(southern suburbs)

**East Coast & Midlands
Tourism**
Market House,
Market Square,
Mullingar, Co Westmeath
www.eastcoastmidlands
ireland.ie; ☎ 044 48650

NATIONAL HOLIDAYS

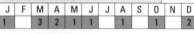

J	F	M	A	M	J	J	A	S	O	N	D
1		3	2	1	1		1		1		2

1 Jan New Year's Day
17 Mar St Patrick's Day
Mar/Apr Good Friday, Easter Monday
May (1st Mon) May Holiday
Jun (1st Mon) June Holiday
Aug (1st Mon) August Holiday
Oct (last Mon) All Soul's Day
25 Dec Christmas Day
26 Dec St Stephen's Day

OPENING HOURS

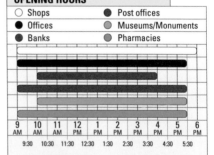

○ Shops   ● Post offices
● Offices   ◐ Museums/Monuments
● Banks   ◐ Pharmacies

9 AM	10 AM	11 AM	12 PM	1 PM	2 PM	3 PM	4 PM	5 PM	6 PM
9:30	10:30	11:30	12:30	1:30	2:30	3:30	4:30	5:30	

In addition to times shown above, some shops open on Sunday. Late-night shopping is on Thursday, with many shops open until 8pm. Most banks close on Saturdays; some remain open till 5pm on Thursdays. City-centre post offices open on Saturday mornings. Pharmacies display a list of pharmacies that open at night and on Sundays.

Museum hours vary according to the season, so always check ahead.

DRIVE ON THE
LEFT

TOILETS
FREE

PUBLIC TRANSPORT

 Internal flights Flights from Dublin to other airports in Ireland are operated by Aer Lingus and Ryanair (▶ 119). Aer Arann (www.aerarann.ie ; ☎ 814 1058) operates the Aran Flyer, with several daily flights between the Aran Islands and Galway.

Trains Ireland has a limited network run by Iarnród Éireann (www.irishrail.ie; ☎ 703 2358), which serves major town and cities. Dublin has two main stations; trains from the north arrive at Connolly Station and trains from the south and west arrive at Heuston Station.

Long-Distance Buses Bus Éireann (www.buseireann.ie; ☎ 836 6111) operates a network of express bus routes out of Dublin serving most of the country (some run summer only).

Urban Transport The city's extensive bus service is run by Dublin Bus (59 Upper O'Connell Street; www.dublinbus.ie; ☎ 872 0000). As there are so many different buses that run across the city, Dublin Bus provides free individual timetables for each route. The Rapid Transit system (DART) runs along the coast from Malahide in the north to Greystones in the south. The LUAS light railway operates from the centre out to the suburbs. There is a range of fare-saving combined travel passes available.

CAR RENTAL

 Car rental in Dublin is expensive. All of the main international car rental companies are represented, however, a car from a local company is likely to be cheaper, but may not allow different pick-up/drop-off points. In July and August it is best to book well ahead.

TAXIS

 Taxi stands are outside hotels, train and bus stations, and at major locations such as St Stephen's Green, Dame Street, O'Connell Street and Dawson Street. Taxis can be hailed on the street but late at night they can be in short supply so you might have to wait in line.
Radio Cabs ☎ 677 2222
City Cabs ☎ 872 7272

DRIVING

 Speed limit on motorways 112kph/ 70mph; dual carriageways: 96kph/60mph

 Speed limit on country roads: 96kph/60mph

 Speed limit on urban roads: 48kph/30mph (or as signposted)

 Seatbelts must be worn in front seats at all times and in rear seats where fitted.

 Random breath-testing. Never drive under the influence of alcohol.

 Lead replacement petrol (LRP) and unleaded petrol are widely available. Many fuel stations in and around Dublin stay open 24 hours, while those in the villages and more rural areas stay open until 8 or 9pm, and open after Mass on Sundays.

 If you break down driving your own car and are a member of an AIT-affiliated motoring club, you can call the Automobile Association's rescue service (1800 667788). If the car is rented follow the instructions given in the documentation; most of the international rental firms provide a rescue service.

At the top is a ruler showing CENTIMETRES (0–8) and INCHES (0–3).

CENTIMETRES

INCHES

PERSONAL SAFETY

• Until recently, street crime was rare in Dublin, but petty crime is on the increase.
• Keep valuables in your hotel safe.
• Pickpockets and bag snatching are prevalent.
• Watch handbags and wallets in public places.
• Avoid Phoenix Park and poorly lit alleys and side-streets after dark.
• Keep cars well secured and avoid leaving property on view.

The national police, called the Garda Síochána (pronounced *shee-kaw-nah*), wear blue uniforms and, in bad weather, yellow raincoats.
Police assistance:
☎ 999 from any call box

TELEPHONES

Public telephone boxes are either blue and cream or the newer glass-booth style, and take coins or phone cards (sold at post offices and newsagents). The Dubin code is 01; dial 10 for national operator assistance and 114 for the international operator. All numbers preceded with 1800 are toll-free.

International Dialling Codes

From Ireland to:

UK:	00 44
USA:	00 1
Germany:	00 49
Netherlands:	00 31
Spain:	00 34
Australia:	00 61

POST

The main post office, in O'Connell Street (☎ 705 7000), opens 8–8 Mon–Sat; for other post offices, hours are generally 9–5:30 Mon–Fri, Sat 9–1. Postboxes are green and stamps are sold at post offices, some newsagents or are available from machines.

ELECTRICITY

The power supply is 240 volts AC. Sockets generally are the UK type, with three square pins. Parts of the Republic also have 2 round pins (Continental type). Overseas visitors should bring a voltage transformer and plug adaptor.

TIPS/GRATUITIES

Yes ✓ No ✗		
Restaurants (if service not included)	✓	10%
Cafés (if service not included)	✓	10%
Hotels (if service not included)	✓	10%
Hairdressers	✓	€2
Taxis	✓	10%
Tour guides	✓	€2
Cinema usherettes	✗	
Porters	✓	€1
Cloakroom attendants	✓	€1
Toilets	✗	

PHOTOGRAPHY

Best times to photograph: early morning and late evening. Irish light can be dull so you may need faster film eg 200 or 400 ASA.
Where to buy film: most film and camera batteries are readily available in many shops and pharmacies.

HEALTH

Nationals of EU and certain other countries can get medical treatment at reduced cost in Ireland with Form E111 (not required for UK nationals), although private medical insurance is still advised and is essential for all other visitors.

EU nationals or nationals of countries with which Ireland has a reciprocal agreement can get dental treatment within the Irish health service with Form E111 (not needed for UK nationals). Others should take out private medical insurance.

The sunniest months are June and July with on average 5–6.5 hours of sun a day, though July and August are the hottest. During these months you should take precautions – cover up, use a good sunscreen and drink plenty of water.

Prescription and non-prescription drugs and medicines are available from pharmacies. When closed, most pharmacies display details of the nearest one that is open. In an emergency, contact the nearest hospital.

Tap water in Ireland is perfectly safe to drink. However, if you prefer to drink bottled water you will find it widely available, though it is often expensive, particulary in restaurants.

CONCESSIONS

Students Students under 18 are entitled to reduced entrance in some museums and galleries. Be sure to carry some form of identification. Holders of an International Student Identity Card can buy a Travelsave Stamp entitling them to travel discounts, including a 50 per cent reduction on Bus Éireann, Iarnród Éireann and Irish Ferries (between Britain and Ireland). Contact your local student travel agency for further details. The Travelsave Stamp can be purchased from USIT (19 Aston Quay, Dublin 2; www.usit.ie; ☎ 602 1777).
Senior Citizens Senior citizens (over 60) are entitled to discounts on transport and most admission fees, on proof of age.

CLOTHING SIZES

Ireland	UK	Rest of Europe	USA	
36	36	46	36	Suits
38	38	48	38	Suits
40	40	50	40	Suits
42	42	52	42	Suits
44	44	54	44	Suits
46	46	56	46	Suits
7	7	41	8	Shoes
7.5	7.5	42	8.5	Shoes
8.5	8.5	43	9.5	Shoes
9.5	9.5	44	10.5	Shoes
10.5	10.5	45	11.5	Shoes
11	11	46	12	Shoes
14.5	14.5	37	14.5	Shirts
15	15	38	15	Shirts
15.5	15.5	39/40	15.5	Shirts
16	16	41	16	Shirts
16.5	16.5	42	16.5	Shirts
17	17	43	17	Shirts
8	8	34	6	Dresses
10	10	36	8	Dresses
12	12	38	10	Dresses
14	14	40	12	Dresses
16	16	42	14	Dresses
18	18	44	16	Dresses
4.5	4.5	38	6	Shoes
5	5	38	6.5	Shoes
5.5	5.5	39	7	Shoes
6	6	39	7.5	Shoes
6.5	6.5	40	8	Shoes
7	7	41	8.5	Shoes

WHEN DEPARTING

- Remember to contact the airport on the day prior to leaving to ensure the flight details are unchanged.
- It is advisable to arrive at the airport two hours before the flight is due to take off.
- If travelling by ferry you must check in no later than the time specified on the ticket.

LANGUAGE

Irish is a Celtic language, probably introduced to Ireland by the Celts in the last few centuries BC. Ireland has two official languages, English and Irish, but everyone speaks English, although you may hear Irish in the Gaeltacht areas of the west and south. You will come across Irish on road signs, buses and trains. Below is a list of some words that you may see while in Ireland, with a guide to pronunciation.

hotel	óstán	(oh stawn)
bed and breakfast	loístín oíche	(lowshteen eeheh)
single room	seomra singil	(showmra shingle)
double room	seomra dúbailte	(showmra dhubillta)
one person	aon duine	(ayn dinnah)
one night	oíche amháin	(eeheh a waa-in)
chambermaid	cailín aimsire	(colleen eym-shir-eh)
room service	seirbhís seomraí	(sher-iv-eeesh showm-ree)

bank	an banc	(an bonk)
exchange office	oifig malairte	(if-ig moll-ir-teh)
post office	oifig an phoist	(if-ig on fwisht)
coin	bonn	(bown)
banknote	nóta bainc	(no-tah bank)
cheque	seic	(sheck)
travellers' cheque	seic taistil	(sheck tash-till)
credit card	cárta creidmheasa	(korta kred-vassa)

restaurant	bialann	(bee-a-lunn)
café	caife	(koff-ay)
pub/bar	tábhairne	(thaw-ir-neh)
breakfast	bricfeásta	(brick-faw-stah)
lunch	lón	(lone)
dinner	dinnéar	(dinn-air)
table	tábla	(thaw-blah)
waiter	freastalaí	(frass-tol-ee)

aeroplane	eitleán	(ett-ell-awn)
airport	aerfort	(air-furt)
train	traein	(train)
bus	bus	(bus)
station	stáisiún	(staw-shoon)
boat	bád	(bawd)
port	port	(purt)
ticket	ticéad	(tickaid)

yes	tá/sea	(thaw/shah)
no	níl/ní hea	(knee hah)
please	le do thoil	(le do hull)
thank you	go raibh maith agat	(goh rev moh aguth)
welcome	fáilte	(fawl-che)
hello	dia dhuit	(dee-a-gwit)
goodbye	slán	(slawn)
goodnight	oíche mhaith	(eeheh woh)
excuse me	gabh mo leithscéal	(gov-mu-le-schale)
how much?	cé mhéid?	(kay vaid)
open/closed	oscailte/dúnta	(uskulta/doonta)

INDEX

Acknowledgements
The Automobile Association would like to thank the following agencies and photographers for their assistance in the preparation of this title:
GUINNESS STOREHOUSE 9b, 15t, 16t, 17t, 18t, 19t, 19b, 20t, 21t, 22t, 23t, 24t, 25t, 26t; HUGH LANE GALLERY 52; ILLUSTRATED LONDON NEWS 64cl; IRISH MUSEUM OF MODERN ART 54c; www.euro.ecb.int 119 (euro notes)
The remaining photographs are held in the Association's own library (AA WORLD TRAVEL LIBRARY) and were taken by STEVE DAY, with the exception of the following:
LIAM BLAKE 44b, 91b; CHRIS COE 51c, 74; SLIDE FILE 17b, 56b, 67b; STEPHEN HILL 50bl, 122t; JILL JENNINGS 75, 76, 77, 78t, 79t, 80t, 81t, 82r, 83t, 84t, 85tr, 86t, 87, 88t, 89tl, 89tr, 90t; CAROLINE JONES 78c, 79b, 80c, 82/83, 83b, 84c, 86/87, 88b, 89c, 90b, 122l; TOM KING 18b; SIMON MCBRIDE 1, 7c, 9ct, 21b, 24b, 25c, 48b; MICHAEL SHORT 2, 6c, 14b, 15c, 38b, 46b, 49l, 50br, 60, 68c, 117t; STEPHEN WHITEHORNE 8b, 13b, 22b, 25b, 27b, 33c, 36c, 45c, 48c, 56tc, 61tl, 73, 112r; WYN VOYSEY 117b; PETER ZOLLIER 80/81, 85tl, 85b

Authors' Acknowledgements
The authors would like to thank the Marketing and Development department at Dublin Tourism, Dublin 2.

Contributors
Contributions to research: Chris Bagshaw   Project editor: Cathy Hatley
Page layout: Nick Otway   Indexer: Marie Lorimer

Dear Essential Traveller

Your comments, opinions and recommendations are very important to us. So please help us to improve our travel guides by taking a few minutes to complete this simple questionnaire.

You do not need a stamp (unless posted outside the UK). If you do not want to cut this page from your guide, then photocopy it or write your answers on a plain sheet of paper.

Send to: **The Editor, AA World Travel Guides, FREEPOST SCE 4598, Basingstoke RG21 4GY.**

Your recommendations…

We always encourage readers' recommendations for restaurants, nightlife or shopping – if your recommendation is used in the next edition of the guide, we will send you a *FREE* AA *Essential* **Guide** of your choice. Please state below the establishment name, location and your reasons for recommending it.

_____

_____

_____

_____

Please send me **AA *Essential*** _____.

About this guide…

Which title did you buy?
 AA *Essential* _____
Where did you buy it? _____
When? m m / y y

Why did you choose an AA *Essential* Guide? _____

_____

_____

_____

_____

Did this guide meet your expectations?
 Exceeded ☐ Met all ☐ Met most ☐ Fell below ☐
 Please give your reasons _____

_____

_____

_____

continued on next page…

Were there any aspects of this guide that you particularly liked? ________

____

____

Is there anything we could have done better? ______________________

____

____

About you...

Name (*Mr/Mrs/Ms*) ______________________________

Address ______________________________

____

______________________ Postcode ______________

Daytime tel nos ______________________________

Please only give us your mobile phone number if you wish to hear from us about other products and services from the AA and partners by text or mms.

Which age group are you in?

Under 25 ☐ 25–34 ☐ 35–44 ☐ 45–54 ☐ 55–64 ☐ 65+ ☐

How many trips do you make a year?

Less than one ☐ One ☐ Two ☐ Three or more ☐

Are you an AA member? Yes ☐ No ☐

About your trip...

When did you book? m m / y y When did you travel? m m / y y

How long did you stay? ______________________________

Was it for business or leisure? ______________________________

Did you buy any other travel guides for your trip?

If yes, which ones? ______________________________

Thank you for taking the time to complete this questionnaire. Please send it to us as soon as possible, and remember, you do not need a stamp (*unless posted outside the UK*).

Happy Holidays!

The information we hold about you will be used to provide the products and services requested and for identification, account administration, analysis, and fraud/loss prevention purposes. More details about how that information is used is in our privacy statement, which you'll find under the heading "Personal Information" in our terms and conditions and on our website: www.theAA.com. Copies are also available from us by post, by contacting the Data Protection Manager at AA, Southwood East, Apollo Rise, Farnborough, Hampshire GU14 OJW.

We may want to contact you about other products and services provided by us, or our partners (by mail, telephone) but please tick the box if you DO NOT wish to hear about such products and services from us by mail or telephone. ☐

The Atlas

Steve Day: *A vibrant St Patrick's Day Parade (above)*

www.theAA.com
The Automobile Association's website offers comprehensive and up-to-the-minute information covering AA-approved hotels, guest houses and B&Bs, restaurants and pubs in the UK; airport parking, insurance, European breakdown cover, European motoring advice, a ferry planner, European route planner, overseas fuel prices, a bookshop and much more.

www.aaa.com
AAA's website offers comprehensive information covering AAA approved hotels and restaurants in the US. In addition, AAA can assist US citizens with obtaining a passport, reservations and tickets for cruise, tour, motorcoach, rail and air travel. AAA provides information on independent or escorted tours for individuals or groups and offers benefits on cruises, tours and travel packages.

The Foreign and Commonwealth Office
Country advice, traveller's tips, before you go information, checklists and more.
www.fco.gov.uk

VISITOR INFORMATION
www.visitdublin.com
www.dublin.ie
www.dublintourist.com
www.eastcoastmidlandsireland.com
www.tourismireland.com

GENERAL
UK Passport Service
www.ukpa.gov.uk

US Passport Information
www.travel.state.gov

Health Advice for Travellers
www.doh.gov.uk/traveladvice

BBC – Holiday
www.bbc.co.uk/holiday

The Full Universal Currency Converter
www.xe.com/ucc/full.shtml

Flying with Kids
www.flyingwithkids.com

TRAVEL
Flights and Information
www.cheapflights.co.uk
www.thisistravel.co.uk
www.ba.com
www.worldairportguide.com
www.aer-rianta.com

www.aerlingus.com
www.ryanair.com
www.aerarann.com
www.easyjet.com
www.continental.com

BUSES, TRAINS AND FERRIES
www.dublinbus.ie
Bus timetables and prices for city buses in Dublin.
www.buseireann.ie
Long-distance buses in the Republic.
www.irishrail.ie
Train timetable and fare information for the Republic.
www.raileurope.com
www.irishferries.com

HORSE DRAWN CARAVANS
www.horsedrawn.in-ireland.net
www.horsedrawncaravans.com

HERITAGE
www.heritageireland.ie
Information on historic sites, castles, gardens and national parks in Ireland.
www.heritagetowns.com
A directory of towns designated Heritage Towns because of their architecture.

WEATHER
www.met.ie
The Irish Meteorological Service (Met Éireann) site gives regional forecasts for the island.

Main road / Hauptstraße / Route principale

Other roads / Sonstige Straßen / Autres routes

Path / Sentier / Pfad

Parking - Information / Parkplatz - Information /
Parking - Information

One-way street / Einbahnstraße / Rue à sens unique

Pedestrian zone / Fußgängerzone / Zone piétonne

Main railway with station / Hauptbahn mit Bahnhof /
Chemin de fer principal avec gare

LUAS light Rail / LUAS Helles Bahn / LUAS Rail Léger

Church / Kirche / Église

Public building / Öffentliches Gebäude / Bâtiment public

Gardens and parks / Gärten und Parks / Jardins et parcs

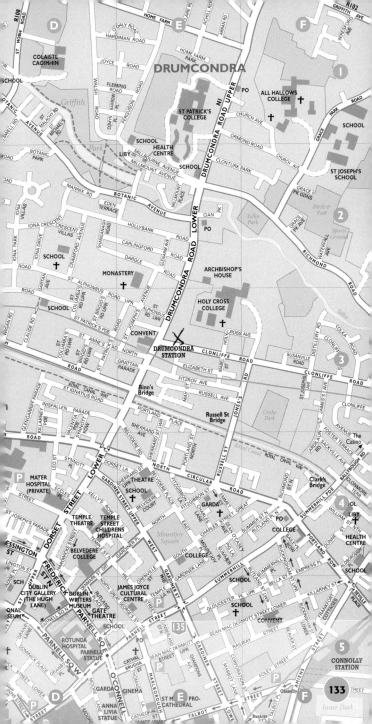

Dublin Street Index